Beyond Pronouns

of related interest

**The Reflective Workbook for Parents and Families
of Transgender and Non-Binary Children**
Your Transition as Your Child Transitions
D.M Maynard
ISBN 978 1 78775 236 8
eISBN 978 1 78775 237 5

The Beginner's Guide to Being a Trans Ally
Christy Whittlesey
ISBN 978 1 78775 783 7
eISBN 978 1 78775 784 4

Becoming an Ally to the Gender-Expansive Child
A Guide for Parents and Carers
Anna Bianchi
ISBN 978 1 78592 051 6
eISBN 978 1 78450 305 5

**Everything You Ever Wanted to Know About
Trans (But Were Afraid to Ask)**
Bryn Tannehill
ISBN 978 1 78592 826 0
eISBN 978 1 78450 956 9

Beyond Pronouns

The Essential Guide for Parents of Trans Children

Tammy Plunkett

Foreword by Mitchell Plunkett

Jessica Kingsley Publishers
London and Philadelphia

First published in Great Britain in 2022 by Jessica Kingsley Publishers
An imprint of Hodder & Stoughton Ltd
An Hachette UK Company

1

Copyright © Tammy Plunkett 2022
Foreword copyright © Mitchell Plunkett 2022
Illustrations by Masha Pimas

Disclaimer: The information contained in this book is not intended to replace
the services of trained medical professionals or to be a substitute for medical
advice. You are advised to consult a doctor on any matters relating to your health,
and in particular on any matters that may require diagnosis or medical attention.

A CIP catalogue record for this title is available from the
British Library and the Library of Congress

ISBN 978 1 83997 114 3
eISBN 978 1 83997 113 6

Printed and bound in the United States by Integrated Books International

Jessica Kingsley Publishers' policy is to use papers that are natural,
renewable and recyclable products and made from wood grown in
sustainable forests. The logging and manufacturing processes are expected
to conform to the environmental regulations of the country of origin.

Jessica Kingsley Publishers
Carmelite House
50 Victoria Embankment
London EC4Y 0DZ

www.jkp.com

To Mitchell, you have changed our lives for the better, and you will change thousands of hearts and minds.

To Mackenzie Neufeld, may this carry your light forward.

Contents

Foreword

My name is Mitchell, the one who inspired my mom to write this book. We thought that I should include a short note for you because my mom likes to say, "not about us without us," so she wanted to make sure to add my voice.

As of writing this foreword, I'm 16 years old. I'm a transgender young man, have been on hormone replacement therapy for about two years, and we're still waiting for top surgery to become an option for me. I love building computers, talking with my friends, and playing video games. I'm also learning how to drive since I just got my learner's license. I want to be an IT technician when I grow up.

When I was younger, I knew that something was off about me and that I wasn't like the other girls. I couldn't figure what was wrong, but it all made sense after learning about transgender people.

I can't speak for all trans kids, but if there is one thing that you, the reader, should take away, it would be that I urge you to support your child unconditionally. It's a hard process, but it can benefit both you and your child since they're feeling vulnerable and sensitive—at least I know I did. One of the things I needed the most when I first came out was someone to acknowledge that my feelings were valid and that we were going to go out and buy boy clothes the next time we were going to the store. I really needed to see a boy in the mirror. I think that starting that social transition is something that trans kids need and parents can easily offer.

The hardest part is dealing with close-minded people, negative comments, and bullies. It mostly happens online, and it happened at my old school. I eventually switched schools, and I was so much happier at the new one.

My mom is one of my best friends, and I think that her writing *Beyond Pronouns* has helped us get closer. She also injects my testosterone shots every week, so that probably also contributes to us being closer. Mom was with me for every single doctor's appointment, psychologist appointment, and discussions about hormone blockers or testosterone. She was a nurse, so she understood the medical terminology that the doctors would talk about, and that helped. I think that's what I needed most, for my mother to be there. She was there when people were rude or discriminatory. She was there when I wanted to change my name and gender on my birth certificate. She was always there for me whenever I needed her, for which I am forever grateful.

My mom eventually started to help others in our community. She launched a group called "Parenting with Pride" and spoke to other parents about supporting their gender-diverse children in our area. She also mentored parents of trans kids. I know that my mom is most happy when she's writing, so I am proud to see this book come to life.

Mitchell Plunkett

Acknowledgments

Sending my biggest thank you to my closest consultant and a dear friend, Kiersten Mohr. Can you believe we have co-led Parenting with Pride for more than four years? Those meetings and your generous sharing of your knowledge and experience have shaped both my understanding and much of what I share in this book. I am beyond grateful to have you in my life. Thank you for your mental health expertise and friendship, Candice Kutyn. Much gratitude to Rebecca Niederlander for sharing the gender-diverse experience in the United States and pointing me towards the research in giftedness and exceptionalism in the transgender population.

Thank you for your forever kind guidance, Andrew James and the JKP editing team.

A book is never written in isolation. So, I want to thank my earliest cheerleaders, Nancy Livingstone, Michelle

Weger, Dr. Wendy Rice, and my first readers when the manuscript was in its infancy, Zoey Duncan, Helene Diotte, Dana Goldstein, and Karen Parnham.

Finally, none of this is possible without my family. Rod, thank you for your undying support in writing this book and your unending support on this journey with Mitchell. You have held my hand and reminded me to breathe for so many years. I couldn't do it without you. Thank you for allowing me to have my blinders on for a while, Sarah, Victoria, and Andy. All those years of watching your mom sitting at the computer have paid off. Use them as a lesson to follow your dreams. Mitchell, to say none of this is possible without you sounds redundant considering the subject matter. But seriously, this book exists because you have kept asking me if you could read the next chapter. I have been so profoundly proud of you and your bravery and authenticity, and all I want is to make you equally as proud with this book. Thank you for trusting us with your truth.

Introduction

Welcome to your safe space.

If you're the parent of a child who just came out as transgender, a thousand questions are swirling in your mind, and a confusing mix of emotions sits heavy on your chest. I know just what you're going through because my own child, raised as a girl, told me he was transgender when he was eleven years old. This book is meant to answer some of your questions and help you understand that those emotions are absolutely okay.

First, I want to address what parents don't hear often enough: you're doing the best you can with the knowledge you have now. You love your child, and your child loves you. How many of us go down the rabbit hole of a Google search after our child comes out just to feel much worse about ourselves at the other end? I felt like a failure for not knowing my child well enough to know sooner. It's easy to beat yourself up for misgendering your child when you used a different pronoun for the past five, ten, even twenty-five years. I wrote this book to be a positive counterbalance to all those feelings. I'm not going to lecture you on "the right way" to be an ally or shame you for not knowing the latest acronym or terminology. This is your safe space.

Our story

Once upon a time, I would have described my family as a blended family with three girls and a boy. After a relatively peaceful divorce, I remarried, bringing along my two daughters and quickly adding a happy, loving, curly-blonde-haired girl followed by an adored, much-celebrated, red-haired boy. We faced challenges, like most families, but managed to bounce back and grow over time. The whole family could always depend on the two youngest kids to bring a sense of joy and balance through anything.

The joy and brightness dimmed and were eventually completely overshadowed by anxiety and depression when our third child started puberty a week before turning ten. We struggled to find the cause for this about-face in our child's mood and behavior to no avail. Suddenly, we were raising a shell of the person who used to fill our every day with happiness.

Then one day, I found a journal on my bed in which our third child came out as transgender. Throughout this book, I'll share our family's story as it unfolded from that point, the parts that helped us connect and feel safe, and the parts that, with hindsight, time, and research, I would have done differently. What I can tell you right away is that today our transgender son, Mitchell, is back to his joyful and bright self. He has brought our family closer and taught us all the value of self-exploration and authenticity, and we're all the better for being on the transformation journey with him.

What does "transgender" even mean?

There are many misconceptions about being transgender so let me dispel a few myths right now. The biggest question you might face as the parent of a transgender child is, "How can a child be transgender?" and that's usually a result of blurring the lines between gender and sexuality. It comes from the days of the past when TV and movies showed cross-dressing as a sexual fetish. If you look at it through a sexuality lens, it will seem odd for a child to be transgender. But nothing could be further from the truth. Gender identity has *nothing* to do with sexuality. Gender is formed in the mind and is a concept a child grasps in early childhood. It has nothing to do with sexual desire or orientation. It's been said that sexual orientation is who you sleep with, and gender identity is who you are when you wake up in the morning before you assume the roles society has constructed for you.

Your child's gender identity is how they think about themselves. Your doctor or midwife announced your child's sex by looking at the external genitalia between their legs. Your child's gender expression is how they like to dress, style their hair, speak, and move their body. Your child's romantic and sexual attraction is independent of these other factors, all of which are on a continuum and not necessarily a male/female or gay/straight binary.

Many terms are used in the world of gender diversity, and this new language can be overwhelming. I follow a guideline of allowing people to make mistakes in terminology when they don't know better, because there was a time I also didn't know better. However, I do offer the correct terminology in this book for the sake of our children who can be hurt by those mistakes. Here are a few terms I will use and what they mean.

Transgender, gender diversity, cisgender: Transgender people have a gender identity or gender expression that differs from the sex and subsequent gender they were assigned at birth. Transgender, often abbreviated as "trans," is an umbrella term. Gender diversity is also an umbrella term encompassing anyone who is not cisgender; cisgender means identifying with the gender one was assigned at birth.

Transgender is an adjective, not a verb. Therefore, someone is not "transgendered" just like someone is not "Latinoed" or "gayed." "Transsexual" is an old term that you sometimes still see in medical texts and refers to someone who has had gender-affirming surgery. But, as you will read later, a transgender person doesn't need to have surgery to be transgender.

Non-binary and genderqueer: Non-binary and genderqueer refer to a spectrum of gender identities that are not exclusively masculine or feminine, meaning identities that are outside the gender binary of male and female. Non-binary identities can fall under the transgender umbrella since many non-binary people identify with a gender that is different from their assigned sex. Other terms for non-binary are enby, from the abbreviation NB, gender fluid, gender creative, gender non-conforming, and agender.

Assigned female (or male) at birth; AFAB, AMAB: Sex assignment (sometimes known as gender assignment) is the discernment of an infant's sex at birth. In most births, a relative, midwife, nurse, or physician inspects the genitalia when the baby is delivered, and sex is assigned without the expectation of ambiguity. An assignment may also be done before birth through prenatal sex discernment, with ultrasound, for example.

It is important to note that scientifically there is more than only male or female. You will hear from ill-informed people that there are only XX chromosomes for girls and XY chromosomes for boys. But that's not accurate. First, most of us never have our children's DNA tested and assign gender on genitals alone. Also, there are Intersex individuals who can have both of what we categorize as male and female reproductive and sexual anatomy. The acronyms AFAB and AMAB are being used instead of the older FTM (female to male) and MTF (male to female) to move away from assuming that all transgender people fully transition along the binary. I also want to assert that it is pretty rare that anyone needs to know about your child's biology besides some doctors.

Your kid isn't broken

Quite soon into the Google searches, we all stumble upon the stark statistics that show higher rates of depression, anxiety, suicidal ideation, self-harm, and substance abuse among LGBTQIA+ youth. It's so important to know that these challenges are often due to the stigma and lack of acceptance that the community faces and are *not* an absolute that comes with being transgender. *Gender diversity is not a mental illness.* Even though the Diagnostic and Statistical Manual of Mental Disorders, 5th Edition (DSM-5) lists gender dysphoria as a diagnosis and that diagnosis can be required in some jurisdictions for medical or surgical intervention, most professionals do not label transgender individuals as mentally ill. However, transgender people, like everyone else, can face mental health challenges and neurodiversity. As you would with any child, you need to address their mental health with the right professional help. But know that mental wellness is protected by having at least one affirming parent, and this whole book is about supporting you, the parent or caregiver, so that you can help your child.

What to expect after your child comes out

Another misconception is that transgender individuals all take hormones or have surgery as adults and that grade schoolers have gender-affirming surgery. It is important to realize that with children and early teens, there won't be medical intervention five minutes after they tell you they are transgender, and they don't start cross hormones right away after coming out either. Initially, there is only a social transition. The social transition is what this book covers, along with a final chapter that takes a sneak peek at the future possibilities.

You'll often hear that transition starts with you affirming the gender of your child. That means you're giving them time to explore the gender that makes them most comfortable, which may be the opposite of how they were identified at birth, or they may assume no one particular gender, a non-binary identity.

A social transition means using the pronouns that your child feels comfortable with and using the name your child has chosen, or if you are lucky, that you get to choose with your child. It also means changing their clothes, the color of their bedroom décor, possibly their backpack, their swimsuit, their sports gear, and more. Nothing highlights how much of our world is gendered as undertaking this process!

It's also important to note that sometimes transgender kids only want to explore their gender identity in private, in their room or at home. They just aren't ready yet to face the questions from the outside world because they want to be sure themselves. Rightfully, there's a lot of processing that has to go on for a transgender person. Sometimes. And other times, the child just knows. They are who they are, and they're ready to assert themselves in the world 24/7 everywhere they go. There is no predetermined timeline to the social transition, and you can't push your child into exploring longer or coming out publicly sooner. You will see this idea often in this book: let your child take the lead.

In the spirit of allowing my child to take the lead, I want to let you know that my transgender son, Mitchell, is involved in and championing the writing of this book. Further, he has permitted me to use female pronouns when telling the stories of who I knew him to be before he transitioned. We have agreed to do this to help you, the reader, follow along in anecdotes. In our everyday life, Mitchell is fully viewed as my son, and we only use male pronouns when we address him.

Now, back to you and how this book will serve you. If your child has just come out to you as transgender, the next hundred days will be filled with many decisions and changes, and not all of them will happen linearly in the way the chapters are laid out in a book. That's okay. Feel free to skip ahead to the topic you need.

This book is meant to empower you as parents, grandparents, or caregivers, acknowledge your journey, and arm you with the knowledge you need to support your child.

This is an ode to the love we share for our children and how we want the best for them. It's a nod to the monumentally important role supportive parents play in the success of a transgender child. It's also a frank look at the unique emotional journeys that we come to terms with behind closed doors and away from our child's awareness.

Chapter 1

∽

Addressing Your Own Feelings

I once thought I was one of the most liberal and progressive people I knew. A feminist to the core, I always fought for human rights and stood firm against prejudice of many kinds. I often said I would never have issues if my children told me they were gay or lesbian. It never crossed my mind that I might have to react to my child telling me they were transgender. Do you remember how, before you had children, you thought you had all the answers about how to be a good parent? And then you became a parent and finally understood some of your own parents' misgivings. We all think we know how we will react to life's curveballs until life truly happens to us.

My third baby was born at home surrounded by my daughters, mother, husband, and two midwives with our beagle, Daisy, howling in the distance. It was a relatively easy birth (as easy as a natural birth goes, I guess), and the minute she popped out, we all looked at the external genitalia and announced, "She's a girl!" in the same way millions of children are assigned their genders at birth throughout the world. For nine-and-a-half years of my child's happy childhood, it never crossed my mind that she was anything but a girl. I dressed her in cute dresses, put her blonde curls up in pigtails, and loved how she sang along with Barbie movies. She later grew to get along better with the boys in our neighborhood, was most comfortable in jeans and a t-shirt, and loved video games. She had what we all thought was a good childhood. And then she started menstruating, and it was like a dark cloud descended on her, making her, and by extension the whole household, absolutely miserable.

We all suffered through months of trying to figure out what was going on. I had raised two other girls through puberty, and this was nothing like what we'd experienced before. We went to a psychologist, had neurological testing, tried equine therapy, energy healing, you name it, and none of it helped us find that happy-go-lucky, empathetic sweetheart of a child we once knew. Instead, we had a child who had developed severe anxiety with panic attacks, was being suspended from school for getting into fights, let her hygiene lapse, and avoided as much social contact as possible.

In an effort to give my daughter a means of communicating what was bothering her, I created a mother-daughter journal that we could each write in and pass along to each other. While I had made a few entries myself, it remained largely empty. Then one day, about a year-and-a-half into thinking this turmoil was our new normal, I found the journal on my bed with an entry from my daughter that said, "I would like to take testosterone like transgender people take."

This is where, in my imagined stellar handling of my child coming out to me, I was supposed to celebrate with him and do everything possible to make his transition an incredible experience. I see it now on social media all the time: well-produced gender-reveal videos for someone's twenty-three-year-old kid or newspaper clippings announcing a rectification of a birth announcement fifteen years later, "Oops we got it wrong, she was a girl all along!" There was none of that. I closed the journal and hid it under my pillow and took my sweet time to even address the subject with my husband, let alone with my child.

Overwhelmed

The news that your child is transgender, whether it is welcome news or not, inevitably leads to many questions. It's easy for a sense of overwhelm to consume you. What does this mean for them physically? What does this mean for them legally? What does this mean with regards to their schooling, relationships, and spiritual life? The questions keep circling in your mind at lightning speed.

Whether it takes you a week or a year to cycle through all of the potential emotions that can arise from your child coming out as transgender, the most important piece to consider is how you're facing and dealing with those emotions.

I don't care if our children are five years old or thirty-five years old; they cannot be our emotional supporters while we process this. Never. It doesn't matter if all your processing is positive, rainbows and sunshine. Your child has enough on their mind to process without you imposing your feelings and drowning theirs out. It is not up to your child to inform and educate you, even if they are adults. It is not up to your child to console you. It is not up to your child to play along with your coming-out party plans if that's not where they are yet on their journey.

While the feelings that we face can be overwhelming, we are the grown-ups with the fully developed prefrontal cortex, and we have to find a support system outside of our child to help pick apart that overwhelm into bite-sized pieces we can digest. You can do this with a supportive spouse, a trusted friend, a coach, a counsellor, or a therapist. There will be resources throughout this book pointing to places where you can find safe and affirming support as a parent.

I often say that I processed my son's transition in my own proverbial closet. I hid my doubts, guilt, anger, and sadness from him and the rest of the world while allowing a select few individuals into my safety bubble. Once I was ready to emerge, there was no limit to my advocacy for my son and other transgender children. But first, I needed to ground myself in a deeper knowledge of our family's truth and undying love.

You, too, will become more confident in your advocacy as you become more familiar with this journey. Start by building your safe group and adding people to that group to expand it. Eventually, you and your child will have so many people in your closet you'll have to bust it wide open.

Shame and guilt

If you look at the media landscape, you will find one of two types of parenting articles and blogs for parents or caregivers trying to support a transgender kid. The first is the ultra-accepting parent narrative that shows mom and dad championing their child with a between-the-lines message of, "Don't you dare cross my child, or I'll cut you." The second is the judgmental parent narrative, the parent who disowns and kicks their child out, leading to the staggering statistics of homeless LGBTQIA+ youth and blood-curdling data on suicide attempts by transgender youth. I didn't feel like I fell into either of those parental narratives. I loved my child and would stand by him no matter what, but I also didn't understand what it meant that he was transgender and how I could have missed it all this time.

I felt shame for having doubts about what my child was articulating. How could a child be so sure? How could I doubt him? I still feel shame for negotiating with him and asking him to consider being a "butch lesbian" instead of transgender. I felt guilt for being concerned about what this would look like to others, how they would judge me as a parent and judge my child. You might also be running through a list of people in your mind that you really don't want to have to talk about this with—people you don't want to have to face.

For now, put those people at the bottom of your contact list. You might need to keep a very tight circle of friends and family at first while you learn more about your child and this journey.

Fear

Once I shared the news with my husband, we both grappled with a whole lot of fear. Our child came out as transgender right when North Carolina was in the news about a battle over transgender people's use of public washrooms. The news coverage was brutal. We were terrified that our child would be attacked for going to the "wrong" toilet.

Our fears spiraled in all directions. Our family is not particularly tall to begin with, and Mitchell stopped growing when he hit his first puberty, so we knew he would always be a short man. Would he get beaten up because of that? Would he be targeted because he didn't appear as masculine as society deems acceptable? We worried that he would have a more difficult time finding a job one day. Would he be discriminated against when he put in applications for an apartment? Will he ever be able to find a spouse who will love him just as he is?

Most of these questions showed our socialization and preconditioning in the world of stereotypes for men and women. Our fears highlighted the transphobia that we were too close to see for ourselves. If you told me I was intolerant of transgender people when my son came out, I would have completely disagreed. I didn't judge other people. I only wanted to protect my child. Today, I realize that wanting to protect my child from being transgender was, in essence, saying that there was something wrong with being transgender. At the very least, we were acutely aware that society at large thought there was something wrong with being transgender and, therefore, something wrong with our child.

There is a concept called Social Identity Theory in the psychology domain, which is all about how humans categorize things to help systematize our thoughts. We automatically put things into categories so that we don't have to think about them anymore, and that works for objects such as fruits and birds as well as for people. I can tell within a split second that a banana is a food that I can eat, and a hummingbird is a beautiful flying creature—that I don't eat.

In the context of gender, those of us who have grown up in North American and European cultures categorize people as female or male within a glance. If you see an individual in a dress with long hair, make-up, and earrings, you will assume that they are female, and you're probably going to think that they're attracted to men. There is a social expectation for how genders present, and a bias in our society towards heterosexuality. We normalize being straight and looking distinctly like a man or a woman, and everything else is considered the exception.

The social aspect arises in this theory because we also categorize people into in-groups like us and out-groups that are not like us. It is pretty unconscious, as you look to others for similarities around any number of things such as your faith, your gender, your race, your political party affiliation, what university you attended or not, the neighborhood you grew up in, on and on. We also unconsciously categorize "others" into out-groups in a primitive game of "stranger danger."

When you stop to think about it, it's easy to see a whole lot of diversity within any of your in-groups. A fan club can have different professions, like different foods, have different styles but all cheer on the same sports team. The challenge is that we paint out-groups with the same brush. I grew up in Quebec, Canada, at the height of the language wars. My mother tongue was English, but I had a French last name and attended a French school. I felt like I had one foot in each camp and was naturally accepted by the English minority and readily accepted by the French. The social disputes between the languages have a long history, and each group holds negative stereotypes. I grew up being told that the out-group French people were uneducated and lower class, and I saw no diversity in that group until I went out into the world as a young adult and found French scientists, athletes, artists, entrepreneurs, and doctors.

The same applies to gender diversity. I was raised to "other" gender diversity. It was an out-group for me. I painted the whole group as gay men cross-dressing as a fetish. I didn't realize the wide variety within the community. In my fear, I didn't see that my son could have any profession, have a family if he chooses that for his future, and find peace and happiness as a trans man one day.

Included in our fear was the fear that this could all just be a phase, a call for attention or the drama of preteens. Heaven knows I had seen my share of drama with my two daughters when they were young adolescents. We didn't understand what we were facing, and it was awfully easy to fall into the trap of confirmation bias as we read about a rise in youth coming out as transgender and dismissing it as a mere trend.

Doubt

How can you trust your child to know they are transgender? How can you tell if it's just a phase? How can you trust that it's not just the latest cool thing to do?

My second daughter does not like kale. I have presented it to her a thousand different ways and asked her to taste it again every time, but she has known from a very young age that she will not eat kale. I trusted that she knew that she didn't like it at seven years old, no matter how much I love it myself. So at what point do I go along with her preference and offer spinach or broccoli instead? I want to be a good mom and take care of her nutritional needs, so when do I accept that my child knows she won't eat kale?

My children have all shown preferences for colors and flavors and types of music and styles of clothes and sports and activities at different stages of their lives, and I let them lead the way on those things. Yet, we question whether we can trust that our child knows what expression of their gender is most comfortable. This is because the social implications of our child coming out as LGBTQIA+ are far bigger than if my son chooses to play the guitar instead of the cello. The reality is that we live in a world that is very much categorized as male and female, and it is also assumed that if you present as female or male, your body parts match that binary.

What happens if you trust your child to know what gender they are more comfortable expressing? Being a former nurse, my first fear was the medical implications. Changing genders to me meant hormone therapy and surgery, which sounded barbaric when I felt that I had a healthy child. The good news for parents of gender-creative children or gender non-conforming teens is that it is not true that gender diversity automatically implies hormones and surgery. Nothing has to be permanent in the beginning.

Your child can dress as the gender with which they are most comfortable. It's just clothes, and a wardrobe can be switched back at any time and any age. If your child is older and flirting with puberty or just entered puberty and it is causing them distress, you can talk to your doctor about puberty blockers (more on this later). They're reversible, and delaying puberty gives them more time to explore their gender identity. If you are convinced this is a phase or something cool to do, you can ride it out.

I also had concerns about the social implications. Let's face it, not everyone in our society is super accepting and enthusiastic about people who are "different." Trusting that my son was indeed a boy, allowing him to dress like a boy and to change his name and pronouns was difficult. Even if this wasn't permanent, even if I was hoping that we were riding out a phase, doing so in public was a big commitment to bravery, courage, and authenticity. Sometimes, scary experiences are worth it. In the end, my son's mental health far outweighed what other people thought of me.

You also have to ask yourself what happens if you don't trust your child. The mental health implications are undeniable. After my child settled down from a relatively short episode of suicidal thoughts, I asked the therapist in the emergency room how I could tell if my son was truly suicidal or just trying to get out of school and away from the relentless bullying he was facing there. Her advice was always to believe there is a suicide risk because if I didn't, and he was genuinely suicidal, I couldn't take back my decision to ignore his plea for help.

I'm not going to list the terrifying rate of suicide attempts by transgender youth here, mainly because they vary from one study to the next. I will be very clear that the rates of depression and anxiety experienced by transgender youth are related to facing stigma from family, friends, and the community at large. If you don't trust that your child knows in their heart that they are a different gender than what they were assigned at birth, you risk damaging their self-esteem. How would you like to live the rest of your life being told that something fundamentally true about yourself that you know to your core has to be hidden and denied? Would you feel depressed and anxious, and live in fear of having that secret show up unexpectedly as you go about your everyday life? Is that the future you want for your child "in case it's a phase"? Of course not. I know that you love your child. Otherwise, you wouldn't be reading this book.

Something that's often referred to in the world of transgender children when parents (or others) ask, "How can we trust a child to know?" is the concept of "insistent, persistent, and consistent." Once your child shares their true gender and is insistently, persistently, and consistently showing up authentically as such, you can trust they are who they say they are. Is there a possibility that a teen is looking for negative attention or going through an exploratory phase? It's possible. I'm sure glad I outgrew my Madonna-lookalike phase, my black-wearing emo phase, and my grunge phase. Gender expression can be transient, just like our chosen style, but identity is not. A transgender person is not going through a phase.

Of course, I am privileged with the experience of being a few steps ahead on this path. I see the difference in my child since we embraced transition. Mitchell's school grades are back to excellent, he thrives in his music lessons, he has true friendships, and there is a spark in his eyes that had been dimmed for years. His happiness and contentment have been worth the social implications, and I would do it all again.

Confusion

After our son first came out and before we had a real discussion with him or the rest of the world, my husband and I had each other and the internet to help us unravel the mystery that was gender transition. For a while, we reinforced for each other that, "this just couldn't be real because..." and we would list off all of the reasons our child falsely thought he was transgender. She never had issues wearing dresses as a little girl—but she'd been quite the tomboy since she was eight. She never had any interest in sports growing up—but she loved to play with the boys and made an amazing machine-gun sound effect.

Then, the more we talked about it, the more we were

able to see subtle signs that could have easily been ignored: every Halloween costume since she was old enough to choose what to wear was a male character, she got into trouble at school for not fitting in with the girls and would rather hang out with the boys, every time she played video games, she always chose a male avatar.

We really wanted to tell ourselves that this was coming out of left field and that we'd never had any indication that we were raising another son. But the reality was that our child was just very good at assuming the role society imposed on him. From the time Mitchell was born, he was told he was a girl. He didn't know that gender diversity was a thing, that he could do anything but the role of a girl he was taught, so he went along with the illusion. Also, when he first started to know that being a girl didn't quite fit him and that there was an option to be his authentic self, he still had to come to terms with the fact that the whole world wanted and expected him to assume that girl role we gave him at birth.

This exhausting assuming of roles is the pain our kids carry around while we worry if they are "trans" enough to affirm them. Our child had undeniably been miserable since estrogen started coursing through his veins. We didn't understand then that gender is something that is formed in the mind and taught to us by society. We didn't understand the feeling of being in the wrong body. At the time, none of our other children or close family ever identified with anything but the gender they were assigned at birth.

Humility

We all have different parenting styles; some of us are more authoritarian while others are more permissive. In either manner, parents are expected to be the guide—the ones with the answers. It was tremendously humbling for me to be facing a situation with my child that I had no answers for. It can be hard to be an adult learner. It takes a lot of humility to be facing a situation where you don't have thirty years of experience or a degree to back up what's ahead of you. I bet that even if you do have a degree in gender studies, you'd probably be a little taken aback when it was your own child challenging their assigned gender.

I have four children. If I have learned anything from raising all of them, it's that there's very little I can control in their lives. While my parenting style has changed over the years from more authoritarian to more permissive, I had to learn that I didn't have as much power as I'd hoped. Of course, I try to instill my values—a sense of civic duty, service to others, being kind. But the reality is that my children are their own human beings. They gravitate towards certain hobbies and music, become friends with people they get along with, and fall in love with those they fall in love with. I would be deluding myself if I thought I could control any part of that.

But when my son came out as transgender, I wanted control. I wanted to prevent the pain of others judging him. I wanted to protect him from bullying. I wanted to avoid complications of a lifetime of medications and surgeries. It wasn't because I didn't love him. I absolutely love my child. But when faced with uncertainty, like many trauma survivors, I cling to control. I've heard from other parents that they have a similar urge for control, whether it's in their environment and outcomes or trying to achieve perfection in other aspects of their life.

What Mitchell needed from me was curiosity. He needed me to listen to his thoughts and feelings. I needed to ask open-ended questions and dance with all the options and possibilities. The world is a much different and much more colorful place when you approach it from the space of curiosity and humility instead of wanting to be the expert and control the situation. Because, in the end, what you can control is much less than you'd imagine. You *can* manage your response. I suggest you respond with the curiosity and the open mind of a lifelong learner.

Being exposed

If my third child had come out to me as a lesbian instead of transgender when he was eleven years old, I'd have been dealing with a different set of circumstances. I concede that I may have had some adjustments to make around the heteronormative hopes and dreams I once had. Still, in all honesty, our everyday life wouldn't have changed that much, and it could certainly have been private information that we chose only to share once she had a same-sex partner.

When you have a child who comes out as transgender, your whole journey is on display. Anyone who knew you and your child before—your extended family, friends, anyone at school, church, or extracurricular activities, your doctor, your dentist, the list goes on and on—they all now know that things have changed. You're using a different pronoun, possibly a new name. They're often dressed differently. You have conversations with the school around the name changes and which bathroom and changeroom to use, discussions with the parents of your child's best friend, conversations with people who have varying degrees of open-mindedness and traditional values.

You soon find out where all these people stand with regards to their ideologies and comfort with gender diversity by the questions they ask. The two reactions that sting the most are the obvious ones of having your fitness as a parent questioned. There were a few people in my life I was worried would call child protective services. The other reaction that made me queasy was feeling like our family was a circus sideshow. Those people would ask prying questions for the entertainment of knowing someone "different" and seemed to want to be friends with us as a badge of honor or as their token transgender friend.

As a middle-class white woman, I've not had to face much discrimination in my life. And still, I worried that people would judge me and judge my family. So I can only imagine the added struggle of intersectionality, which, in my view, is a piling on of ways in which someone can face discrimination or prejudice. For example, being a transgender woman of color is intersectionality, so is being differently abled, not having English as your first language, or living in poverty.

The first time I ever felt the heat of embarrassment rise in my cheeks when "coming out" was very early on as a volunteer for our local Pride organization. I was attending a class on grant applications for non-profits, and the facilitator asked us all to introduce ourselves and our organization. I already felt out of place in a sea of grey-haired people, and I had no idea what people would say or do merely from my introduction. When I said that I was with the Pride organization I figured everyone would assume that I was a lesbian and judge me for being queer. I worried that religious people would think I was evil or that I wouldn't fit in during our session. Nothing bad happened. But those feelings immediately highlighted for me a fraction of what disenfranchised people must feel every day. I was only a volunteer in a position I could quit at any time. Others can't shed their skin color or identity quite as easily.

I found it particularly difficult to educate my friends and family and advocate for my child's needs when I wasn't yet sure of what I was advocating. I wasn't yet sure I understood for myself what I was teaching others. But I trusted my gut to know who to confide in and who to keep on a need-to-know basis. My advice to you is to trust your gut too.

Pride

While we took our time investigating things in our minds, our son took control of his destiny and came out to his teachers, asking to be addressed with male pronouns. He eventually spearheaded his social transition, too, and changed his name to Mitchell. His authenticity and bravery were unwavering, and in many ways, he was the leader charging our family forward in the journey.

We might have been initially reluctant to accept the change that descended over our family, but there were times we were hit with waves of pride. I remember clearly the day my husband and I walked into a restaurant with the two youngest kids in tow and asked for a booth. The hostess turned to Mitchell and said, "Would you like a kid's menu or an adult menu, young man?" Mitchell beamed from being addressed as a boy. I also felt a sense of joy and relief, knowing that this might actually be something we could do. Maybe everyday life would be just fine, and people would think of my child as my son.

My husband shares his own anecdote about when he realized that life raising a transgender son was going to be okay. We were visiting a museum, and an interpreter asked to show our "boys" an exhibit. The gentleman explained the diorama in detail while our boys listened intently, and we parents enjoyed the wave of relief that life could continue as usual.

As time progressed, Mitchell advocated more and more for himself and other kids and teens in our local Pride group. Many of the friends he made remain family friends to this day. He started a Gay-Straight Alliance club at his school, he walked at the head of the Pride parade, and he cheered me on to write about our experience as a family. He reads every blog and article I write and listens to every podcast and video I've been on. His bravery and determination have had a positive impact on many more families than our own.

A transgender person spends forever and a day learning who they are and learning how to assert themselves in the world. I'm proud to have a son who was surer of himself and his identity than many adults in my life, including me.

Sadness

Talking about grief and sadness around your child's transition can be taboo in the public domain and on certain Facebook groups that are more concerned with supporting the transgender child than the parents or caregivers. Some people seem to see an association between acknowledging that you have ambiguous feelings of loss for the child you thought you were raising before transition and an idea that you don't support your child's transition. There was a period when I felt a loss for the daughter I once knew, and it has absolutely nothing to do with how much I support my son today.

I had envisioned a future for my daughter that could no longer come to fruition. I had imagined shopping for a prom dress, watching her dance with my husband on her wedding day, and being there for her when she gave birth to my grandchildren. I had invested eleven years of hopes and dreams for my child's future. I had to grieve the loss of the future I had imagined.

There were many personality traits I had seen in her that I associated with her being a girl; her kindness and helpfulness, her cheerfulness and her giggly nature were things I thought would disappear if she was a boy. I now know none of that is true. Some aspects of our personalities transcend gender. But I had to give myself the grace of having been raised and socialized in a very binary world that assigned not only colors, clothes, and toys to the genders but also dispositions, personality, and character traits.

Then there was the fact that I had to erase part of our family's history by not having pictures of Mitchell pre-transition and not using the name we had so carefully chosen for him when he was born. Sadness always bubbled up when I got notifications on Facebook of the memories "on this day" that showed the girl I adored so much.

Some of you might feel a twinge of sadness, while others

might be overcome with grief. Know that you are not alone in feeling this way. But please don't share these feelings with your child.

Our kids are dealing with enough of a weight on their own; they don't need to carry any guilt for making us sad. I pride myself in having very open communication with my children, and I also have the philosophy of being transparent when I mess up and share my mistakes to show my kids my humanity. But this is different. Sharing this sadness would have crushed my son who himself was dealing with an unreliable precarious acceptance from peers. He already struggled with anxiety and depression; he didn't need the added burden of my sadness and grief. Even if your child is a young adult and seems to be dealing with their transition with ease, your sadness is not for them to soothe or fix; it is not something you need to share with them.

What can you do with all these emotions?

The reality is that most of us parents and caregivers grew up in a binary, heterosexual culture, and most of us were handed a baby who was wrapped in either a pink or blue blanket, and we automatically assumed they would one day marry someone of the opposite sex. It's a shock for many of us to have our children tell us something different from what we assumed from the day we first held them in our arms. The best thing you can do for yourself in that state of shock is to take a bit of time and create some space between what you've been told and your next step.

In an effort to educate yourself, Google, the bookstore, and the library will soon become your best friends. I have included an ample resource section at the end of this book to help with your searches. Of course, be wary of the sources from which you gather your information. There are a lot of new terms and labels to familiarize yourself with, like "demiboy" and "Lunarian non-binary," and there are statistics you will want to know about that I have mentioned earlier, such as homelessness and suicide attempts among transgender teens. I know these statistics can cause us more stress, but they are an important part of the whole picture to keep your kid safe.

Reach out for help from another adult. Your kid needs you, and you also need your own support. Some of your existing friends will be amazing and will listen and empathize, and some will be a source of more stress and non-stop, almost voyeuristic questions—choose who you confide in wisely. There may come a time when you need to speak to a counsellor to help you past the most stressful parts, and there are excellent psychologists who can help you and support you so that you can be an advocate for your child. I found significant benefits in meeting other parents of gender-diverse children, and many organizations offer this support, such as PFLAG and GLAAD, both of which you can find online.

Be compassionate with your child and be compassionate with yourself. It took a monumental amount of bravery for your child to come out to you and be their authentic self. How many of us can say, as adults, that we are our authentic selves? Our kids have a world of judgment to face, and you being their safe place to land is a genuine gift for them. This is not easy on you as a parent! I know. I live it. There's a steep learning curve, and there are so many opportunities to mess up. I've used the wrong pronouns. I've dismissed something that I thought was minor that turned out to be a big deal to my kid. I've had to go through a bona fide grieving process for the daughter I gave birth to, and that's okay. I am compassionate with myself, but most importantly, I don't dump my feelings on my child.

You Time

I want to challenge you to take a few minutes to yourself at the end of each chapter to process what you just read, even if it's as little as one deep breath, to center yourself instead of racing ahead to reactivity and fixing mode. I'm not only an author and a former registered nurse; I am also a certified life coach. Coaching is all about asking questions. It helps people create both big and small changes for themselves by reconnecting to their values. I often say that coaching asks people the right question to get them to find the answers already inside them. So, at the end of each chapter, I will offer you at least three questions to help you process this life change.

My best advice is to find a journal and a nice pen, steep yourself a beautiful cup of tea, and get comfortable exploring these questions. If that little oasis of time isn't available to you, at the very least, open a note on your smartphone and tackle them there.

The more you can be grounded and calm, and purposeful in your actions with your child, the more you can be of service to them and yourself. Allow yourself this You Time for their sake if not your own.

1. What was I taught about gender roles when I was growing up?

2. How does the news of my child being gender diverse challenge the messages I received in the past?

3. What are my core values? How can those values help me support my child?

4. What factors do I feel contribute to my ability to remain curious and flexible when faced with change? How can I apply them now?

Chapter 2

∽

Important Conversations You'll Have with Your Child

You might hear this more than once, but congratulations for raising a child who knows themselves well enough to question their gender identity and for having a relationship that is open enough for them to tell you about it. I'm sure there are many questions that you want to ask your child, but even with the most loving and accepting of parents or caregivers, sometimes your child won't want to talk. That can be a difficult place to sit in, considering all the emotions we covered in the last chapter.

To this day, my son doesn't talk about what he struggled with before realizing that he was transgender or what pointed him towards exploring gender identity. All we know about is a video he watched on YouTube. For our family, it initially seemed that one day we had a daughter, and the next day we had to accept the fact that our child was transgender. Within the first hundred days after our child came out, we had a few conversations one-on-one and we had a few together with my husband. At first, only we knew, and then I spoke with my older daughters and best friend about it, but by the end of those first hundred days, Mitchell had decided to ask his teachers to use male pronouns and assert his male identity to the world.

For the past four years, I have co-facilitated a local peer-led support group for parents of LGBTQIA+ kids, teens, and young adults. My co-facilitator, Kiersten, came up with a great analogy. She said that we have to think about our child's gender-diversity journey as a ride on a bus, and our kids are the ones driving the bus. Your child gets to choose how fast to accelerate the bus as long as it's within the legislated speed limits, which means your child gets to decide how fast they ask to be affirmed socially and medically within the standards of transgender medical care. Your child also gets to choose who they allow on their bus, which means they get to choose who knows about their gender identity, and they get to determine if they are the one to tell certain people or they might ask you to do it for them.

For me, allowing my child to drive the bus was a challenging undertaking. He was only eleven years old, and the idea of having an eleven-year-old in charge of these monumental decisions terrified me. But allow me to reassure you that when your child is young, you get to sit at the front of the bus, right next to them, and help guide them on their journey. Anyone who has taught their teen to drive in real life can relate to the nerve-wracking experience. It's not much different in this analogy, but our teens eventually get the hang of their independence. If your child is a young adult, naturally, you will have less input and may not even be invited on the bus for the beginning of the process. Therefore, it's vital to continue supporting and affirming your young adult and accompanying them on the journey in the ways they so choose.

Secret vs. private

In the introduction, I alluded to the possibility that your child may want to explore their gender at home in the privacy of their bedroom or the privacy of your family and not necessarily come out to the world. This is one of the first conversations that you will want to have with your child, and you want to have that conversation in a way that doesn't make it sound or feel shameful to them in terms of, "Do we want to hide this from the rest of the world?" as if there's something wrong with it. On the other hand, you also don't want to push them in the direction of needing to come out to everyone, which can be a stressful experience. This is, again, a place where you want to let your child take the lead in deciding who needs to know and when.

During this conversation, you'll want to make a clear distinction between secret and private. A secret can have an embarrassing or shameful undertone to it. It can make the child feel like they're doing something wrong if they have to keep it a secret from Grandma or the teacher or the next-door neighbor. However, looking at it from a private perspective, meaning that there are some things that are so special that we only share them with certain people that we trust and are very important to us, can help clarify who they want to tell first and why.

Again, this question of keeping their gender exploration private may appeal to some kids while others are firm in their identity and want to be seen and known for who they are with everyone. Your child might need to be seen as their identified gender to avoid distress and discomfort, even if you might not be completely ready to face the world and the questions that will follow. Tread lightly here if you are trying to buy yourself some time, and be sure that it's not at the expense of your child's wellbeing.

Gender expansiveness vs. gender dysphoria

Keeping the analogy of the bus in mind, your child will be the one in control of what route the bus will take. For example, they may want to take a slow drive through the country roads or a six-lane expressway. As well, your child can start on one route and change their mind to taking a different course. Changing the route doesn't mean they are not gender diverse. It means they want to explore the possibilities on this journey.

Depending on your child's age, another conversation that you might want to have is about establishing any area of distress. Gender dysphoria is a medical term concerning transgender healthcare. It looks different in different individuals but is a sense of unease, distress, or uncomfortableness because their bodies do not match with their gender identities. One of the ways that you can identify gender dysphoria is when your child doesn't want to look at pictures of themselves or in the mirror. They may not want to see themselves naked and not want to take a shower or a bath because they're forced to actually look at their body or even touch their body and body parts that they don't want. They may outright say, "I don't want a penis," or, "I don't want breasts." Some kids shower in the dark, shower partly clothed, or don't shower at all unless forced to do so. Another clue, which was the case for my son, is extreme discomfort with signs of puberty such as menstruation or erections. Before transition, my child had massive issues with menstruation. He hated it, well, she at the time. Not that most people I know love to get their period, mind you, but she would do everything she could to avoid dealing with her period. She hated changing sanitary napkins to the point where there were times when she just wouldn't wear them and would free bleed because she wanted to deny the fact that she had this female biological function.

This distress can be disturbing to parents, too, from the minor frustration of having a smelly kid to the significant worry of seeing your child struggle with their mental health, social situations, or life in general. No parent wants to see their child cutting themselves, starving themselves, or isolating themselves and they can feel helpless to make things better for their kid.

As I look back on our transition journey with Mitchell, the times I wanted to live in denial that I had a trans son weren't always because I was transphobic. Sometimes, I didn't want my child to be suffering the way he did with gender dysphoria. I just wanted the happy and healthy child I had once seen from the outside when he was assigned female. It was the same feeling I grappled with when my youngest child was diagnosed with celiac disease. It had nothing to do with gender. I just wanted the ease of food choices back again. But the reality was that Mitchell lived every day in a gender display that was a complete act for him and did not match what he knew about himself. That is what we urgently needed to fix.

A quick note to add the distinction between gender dysphoria and body dysmorphia. Both stem from the world of psychology. Gender dysphoria is related to being transgender, as it refers to the mismatch between the identity of a person and their sex assigned at birth. Body dysmorphia has to do with a disconnection between what they see in the mirror and reality. A person can see defects that aren't really there or see characteristics as accentuated or distorted. While both of these can be present in a transgender person, most often, we are only dealing with gender dysphoria.

On the other hand, other children are gender expansive

or gender non-conforming without feelings of dysphoria and are content with merely expressing themselves in the gender they are aligned with at that time. They have no issue with having the genitalia of any particular sex, have no problem with any secondary sex characteristics, and are okay with their body the way it is, though they might conceal those characteristics, for example by binding their chest, when they feel like it. They only want to have their gender expressed differently, which means that they want to dress, style their hair, and accessorize a certain way. Some people like to use the term gender creative to describe their identity, meaning they want the creativity of blending genders and picking from both a feminine and masculine wardrobe. Gender expression falls under the umbrella of transgender, but it doesn't mean that they need to change pronouns, though they might choose to, or change their name, though they might choose that as well.

This can also be confusing for some parents, as we live in a very binary world. Having your child say, "I am not a boy, I am a girl," can be easier to conceptualize than having your child say, "I want to be both feminine and masculine or neither depending on how I feel that day. I also want to use they and them pronouns." There are also more and more teens and young adults introducing themselves as she/they or they/he, which can be confusing when we are new to these terms. This means either of the pronouns are acceptable when addressing them, and they usually put the pronoun they are most comfortable with first.

Stealth vs. out

Does your child want to be driving a bus painted in the transgender flag, or would they prefer a bus that blends in with the rest of the traffic? They might want to be stealthy and blend in with the rest of the binary world, or they might want to be out and proud and let their freak flag fly!

Back in the day, say the 1960s and 1970s, there was a phenomenon called parachuting when adults would transition. That was when the transgender person would transition in a whole new city, with a new job, new friends, and a new place to live. They would leave their old life behind and parachute into a new life as their true gender. Think along the lines of a witness relocation program. Since being transgender was so taboo, and in many cases, illegal, it was the only way to transition. Today, some families still choose to do this with their children. Moving to a new school or a new city is one way of avoiding telling anyone that your child is transgender. I should note here that gender-diversity experts do not necessarily recommend this, and part of the reason for that is the shame around carrying a secret, as I mentioned earlier.

That said, before your child develops any secondary sex characteristics, it can be pretty easy to pass as their authentic gender with a new haircut and a change of clothes. In that case, everybody assumes that if you introduce your child as a girl, your child is a girl. There are advantages to doing things this way, because there are fewer uncomfortable conversations, fewer explanations to give, no risk of being judged as a parent for allowing your child to transition, and no chance of your child being judged or bullied. However, all this depends on how attached you are to your old life and how readily you can give up your old relationships.

Personally, I never felt that this was an option for us. Even though, when my child came out, we had just moved across the country and were in a new city with no family and very few friends and every relationship we had was a burgeoning one. When Mitchell came out to us, he had only been at his new school for half a year. Yet, the concept of transitioning in secret felt off to us, especially to Mitchell. He was very adamant that he would transition openly and have everyone know that he is a transgender boy, not only a boy.

In full transparency, though, we did end up having to change schools because of Mitchell's transition. The first school where he initially came out did not handle things appropriately as an administration, and some of the students didn't take his transition well either. We were very disappointed, but in retrospect, they probably didn't know what to do and how to deal with things, and neither did we. When Mitchell started at his new school, he was only known as a boy and only introduced as a boy, and no one except for the principal and a few teachers knew that Mitchell was not assigned male at birth.

Note, it can be very important to some transgender

people to be recognized not as transgender but only as their true identity. For example, they don't want to be introduced as, "my trans son Mitchell," only as, "my son Mitchell." While you may not be relocating your family, as a family, you may choose never to disclose that your child is transgender unless absolutely necessary for medical or legal reasons. This is something to verify with your child because it can cause distress for a child to constantly be "outing" themselves as trans, while others own that distinction with pride and want everyone to know.

Within a few months of attending his new school, Mitchell had made some really good friendships, and he felt like he was lying to his friends by not telling them he was trans. He was also concerned about some crossover of friends from the old school at his extracurricular activities. Some kids who attended his music classes knew him as a girl initially and now knew him as a boy. He didn't want word to get around to the friends at his new school that he was transgender and have them think that he was lying to them. Mitchell talked about it with the principal, who handled the situation with Mitchell, and with us, beautifully.

Before Mitchell came out as transgender, the principal trained the staff and had a three-part workshop for the students to explain what it was to be transgender so that a twelve-year-old wasn't responsible for presenting to a group of grade-seven students what transgender meant. After that, Mitchell came out to his two closest friends with the school counsellor in private, and once that went over well, he came out to the entire class.

Knowing what hurts

Because so many of us parents don't know what it's like to live life as a child or teen who is gender diverse, we may not be clear on all of the little things that can be hurting our child. We can equate this to bugs on the windshield of the bus. A bug can seem like a tiny annoyance compared to hitting a deer or a moose, but if you have enough mosquitoes squashed on the glass, you eventually can't even see through it, and trying to use your wipers merely smears the bugs' guts and makes it worse.

These little things are also known as microaggressions and can pile up into a good amount of pain all day long, every day. This is something that you will want to check in on with your child, because an occasional misgendering won't bother one child, while it can be a harsh blow to another. It might be your only misgendering mishap of the week, but your child may have been misgendered all day long elsewhere, and this one last misgendering could be the one drop of water that makes the vase overflow.

As parents, we might not see how often a child faces a reminder that their gender identity isn't mirrored back to them in the world. As a woman, I have used a men's washroom with a girlfriend at a conference when the line was too long for the women's room, and the men's room was empty. I felt a little naughty, but it didn't kill me. But that was once. I can't imagine having to negotiate the sense of danger of being discovered every single time I need to use the bathroom in a public place. Then there are the times our kids get put into a changeroom before gym class, or a girls' or boys' line-up at school, or when people automatically assume a gender when offering a free toy at a restaurant. We need to ask about all these little hurts that we might overlook.

Religion can be a challenging subject to navigate as a family that falls anywhere on the LGBTQIA+ acronym. Religion might play a considerable part in your family's everyday life before and after disclosure. Depending on what faith your family practices, there are some honest conversations that can be had about how to reconcile religious attitudes towards gender diversity. A trans kid can face an internal battle between what they've been raised to believe about the LGBTQIA+ community through their faith and what they know about themselves. Imagine being told all your life that who you are at your core is bad or sinful. That's a lot to unpack as a preteen! A trans kid also faces what is said in the general public, on the news, and from the pulpit after they come out as transgender.

The mere act of going to church or youth group once or twice a week or attending a religious school every day can be a painful reminder to your child that some people around them believe there is something inherently wrong with them. Those microaggressions add up. As parents, we can convince ourselves that it's only a couple of hours a week or a few times a year during high holy days, hoping our kids just ignore the hard parts for something important to our own identity. Still, we need to understand the cumulative pain our child feels. Some kids just want to avoid church because it's boring, but trans kids might want to avoid church because it's a painful reminder that they are flawed in some people's eyes.

We also need to recognize how much the topic of transgender children comes up in news coverage and on social media posts. Learning about laws that remove their rights to access bathrooms, medical care, and play sports can feel like a slap in the face every time they tune into it. Sadly, once kids are old enough to go online, we might not be able to shelter them from how they are being assaulted and oppressed in the world. So pay attention to how your child talks about the news and how it might be affecting their wellbeing.

Rehearsal and safe spaces

This falls under the driver's education handbook that we all have to study before hitting the road. We can help our kids learn what the different signs mean, and how to fill up the gas tank and check their oil. Stealth or out, either way, your child will need to have some conversations with professionals or other adults in their life and know what to say and how to handle topics about their body and identity.

The first thing you can do as a family is identify who is part of their safe support system. Who are the safe teachers that they can go to when they need help or need to work through a conversation with someone in their school? Who are the safe parents in their group of friends that they can comfortably have conversations with if things are going bad?

You might also want to practice having conversations with your child. These are rehearsal conversations to know how to answer when people ask them pointed questions such as, "Have you had surgery?" or, "Are you a boy or a girl?" Sometimes, those questions are innocently posed by a toddler at an age where categorizing people as boys or girls is very important. But, sometimes, questions are asked by older kids who know the answer and are specifically looking for a reaction. I remember a neighborhood child playing with my youngest son and when referring to Mitchell saying, "He used to be a girl," repeatedly. Finally, after having enough, I spoke firmly with the eight-year-old to say, "Mitchell has never been a girl, and you are not ever to say that again. Mitchell is Anderson's brother, and that's all you need to know." Trust your gut and teach your child to trust theirs. You will know when people are saying things to disparage your child or asking out of curiosity.

Along those lines, you will want to rehearse with your child how to answer gracefully to avoid a question that either of you is not comfortable answering. This was a fine line for me to navigate, as I am a natural teacher who loves to share with others for the benefit of their learning and to convert everyone to transgender allies. But I would never talk about my genitalia or which underwear I wear with my accountant, so there are obviously questions that none of us should have to answer for people who don't fit into our closer private circles. Some ways of avoiding these prying questions are to ask them back to the person asking them, "What private parts were you born with?" You can do this with or without a smile, and they will instantly blush and realize the error of their ways.

Another excellent rehearsal conversation to have with your child is to help them learn when their reserves are low and they need to retreat from stressful situations. You can help your child practice breathing exercises and mindfulness tricks such as the 5-4-3-2-1 Grounding Technique, where you identify five things you see, four things you feel, three things you hear, two things you smell, and one thing you taste. You might also want to develop a family code word for when your kid doesn't feel safe and needs an out of a conversation or situation. I always told my kids, even before Mitchell came out, that if they were in a position that didn't feel safe to blame their need to leave on me, "Tell your friends I am an evil witch who doesn't let you have any fun, whatever you need to save face and get out of there. I have broad shoulders and can carry the blame."

The big "why?" question

The temptation of having your child tell you why they are transgender or where the "idea" came from is monumental. I know. As parents, we want to be sure that this isn't a phase and that we aren't encouraging something that might be nothing. However, you must tread lightly here because this conversation can quickly and easily come across as accusatory or put your child on the defensive for having to justify how they feel and who they are. A great rule of thumb that I learned long ago in my coach training is never to use the question "Why?" but instead start my questions with "What..." First, it avoids the yes/no option and sometimes it magically skirts the "I don't know" answer that teens especially like to use to shut down a conversation. Second, it also allows your child to share what they know, understand, and feel if they don't know why. For example, you can ask, "What is it like when you look in the mirror? What does it feel like when someone mistakes you for a boy (or a girl)? What do you like the most about your gender?"

While on the topic of why, I want to cover this being a fad that your child picked up from their group of friends. I hear this concern from many parents that I work with either one-on-one or in support groups—that because their child joined a cosplay club or Gay-Straight Alliance at school, it became a fad to be non-binary or transgender. But in reality, your child was attracted to hanging out with the drama club or the Gay-Straight Alliance because those were their people. My youngest son is not interested in contact sports. He is not going to start hanging out with the football team suddenly. Also, the Gay-Straight Alliance at school or in your community is a place for kids to explore who they are while feeling psychologically safe. It's where they try on new names and identities and practice with teachers or counsellors how to talk to their parents or grandparents about their most profound realizations. It is not a place where children are converted to becoming LGBTQIA+. It is a place where children feel safe enough to be themselves.

Questions you can ask

This whole book unpacks these questions in a wider context, but I also wanted to provide a list that my son and I came up with together covering what I asked and some questions he wished I would have asked in the beginning. Might I also suggest my ninja parenting trick of having these conversations alone on a long drive if possible. There's something magical about avoiding eye contact and the fact that your child is restrained and can't just walk away from the conversation, which helps with opening up. But do respect the limits of your child's discomfort and don't push a conversation that is distressing them. Here are some questions to get you started.

- What name and pronouns should I use when I talk about you?

- Do you want me to use that name and those pronouns outside of our house?
- Who can I talk about this with?
- What do you need from me to feel more comfortable?
- Are you comfortable in your body, in your clothes, in your style, and in your room?
- Are you thinking of hurting yourself?
- Are you overwhelmed with sadness or fear, and does it bother you many hours a day and many days of the week?
- Do you want to talk to an adult transgender person who has lived a similar experience?

Be ready to get an "I don't know" to some of these questions. I have learned on this journey that there are external processers and internal processers. Some people need to think about a question and mull it over internally for a while before answering. In contrast, others need to talk or act things out and try them on before they know what they want.

Again, this is a conversation you'll want to have gently with your child so as not to steer them in any one direction. You do want to know if body dysphoria is driving their transition to address those feelings. You also don't want to jump to the foregone conclusion that your child will one day need hormone therapy if they are only wanting to be gender expansive in how they dress and want to explore living in the opposite gender than what they were assigned at birth.

I understand that in the beginning, when our minds are newly absorbing all of this, it can be confusing enough on its own to know that someone can identify as the opposite gender from what they were assigned at birth. It's also a lot to unpack that there is a whole continuum between male and female. Be gentle with yourself.

You Time

It's time for you to take a deep breath and center your-self to incorporate what you just unpacked about your gender-diverse child and yourself. So, grab your journal and dive into these questions.

1. What has real meaning for me from what I've read about gender?

2. What surprised me and what challenged me with regards to all the relationships in our life?

3. What's missing from this picture so far? What do I need more clarity about?

4. How can I find a gentle and affirming way to learn more of what I need?

Chapter 3

∽

What and When
to Tell Whom

Building on the conversation earlier about the difference between secret and private, let's look at the levels of intimacy and importance of certain relationships. This exploration might offer some clarity on why your child is more comfortable telling certain people about their gender diversity than others. Remember, they have control of opening and closing the door on their bus and get to choose who gets on and where they sit.

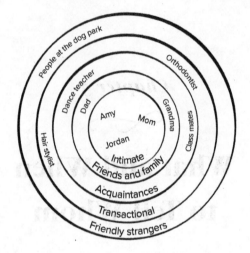

Circles of Relationships

Many different disciplines talk about the circles of relationships and draw a graphic that looks like a bullseye. The circle's center is your most intimate relationships and is usually reserved for a few people that you love. For some, this is a parent or best friend, or a romantic partner later in life. The next ring out is the friendship or family circle and can include siblings, grandparents, and close friends. The next ring out is the acquaintances' circle, and this consists of the people you know, such as your neighbors, classmates, teammates, and co-workers. The next ring out is the transactional circle. This includes people you have a paid relationship with, so anyone you exchange money with, such as a tutor, a hairdresser, or an eye doctor. Finally, the last circle is the stranger that you might smile and nod to as you walk your dog but otherwise have no relationship with at all. Go ahead and draw this out for your child. Place them in the center and then show the relationships they have in the appropriate circles moving outward. Let them show you who are their closest and least intimate people.

One of my favorite quotes is from Michelle Obama's book *Becoming* (2018, p.270), "I've learned that it's harder to hate up close." I use this as a guiding principle every time I share our story to show people that my son is a human being and not just a letter on an acronym. It is easiest for people closest to us, who know Mitchell intimately, to accept and love him as he is. Strangers may not have that history with us, and many don't even need to know about my son's journey, but when we do dare to be open with them, it draws them in closer.

That being said, your child will want different people to know they are transgender first, depending on their developmental stage and comfort levels. In the early stages, parents are very much the closest and most intimate relationship. Your child might also place high importance on being accepted by their grandparents if they are a massive part of your child's life. Whereas in older stages, such as the preteens and teens, your child is developmentally forming an identity outside of their parents. This is also a stage where teens might have come out to their friends before coming out to you. This could be because they have included their friend in their most intimate circle. It could also mean that they assess the risk of losing that friendship as being less devastating than losing their relationship with you.

Remember this as you start to evaluate who to share your child's journey with—your child might not want to tell certain people, such as a close grandparent, because they don't want to risk losing that relationship. Or they may tell their most precious relationship first for the additional support.

Who needs to know?

It will feel like everyone needs to know why your child is dressed differently and using a new name and that no one needs to know all at the same time. Remember that, in fact, not everyone needs to know. And extremely few people need to know anything about your child's body. Not only will your child want to evaluate who to tell according to the intimacy and value of the relationship, as a parent or caregiver, so will you. Go back to the circles of relationships that you drew for your child and draw one for yourself too. Who can you depend on to support you, no questions asked? Who can you put off talking to when you feel more secure in understanding what's going on with your child? You will be faced with questions that people may not ask children but will feel empowered to ask you. Be prepared for that the same way you are preparing your child. All of this hinges on how well people knew your child before social transition and how well your child passes to strangers and mere acquaintances.

Passing is a term you will hear a lot in the transgender community, and it refers to how well your child appears as the gender with which they identify. This can be done quickly with younger kids, as it only involves new clothes and a new hairstyle for most. However, as a transgender child ages and approaches puberty, their body can betray their gender identity as the wrong secondary sex characteristics appear. For example, while his peers might be getting hairier and have their voices drop, a trans boy would be dealing with menstruation and breast development, and while a trans girl's peers develop breasts and start their periods, she might be dealing with thicker peach fuzz.

The gender of your child will also have an impact on public acceptance when they're not entirely passing yet. In our society that considers everything feminine as a less-than and weakness—ask any woman or effeminate gay man—it might be more challenging for your teen to be accepted as a girl if they were assigned male at birth. They may face more teasing for the very nature of expressing femininity. At the same time, it is more acceptable to be a "tomboy" as a person assigned female at birth—to wear boy shorts, sports shoes, and flannel shirts and like to play soccer with the boys.

The harsh reality is that the sooner your child can pass and not arouse suspicion from strangers, the fewer people you will feel obligated to talk with about your child's gender diversity. Before having a legal name change, my rule of thumb was to only disclose to people who needed to have Mitchell's legal birth name, for example, anything medical or that involved health insurance, tax documents, or permanent school records. I also only disclosed information about his body to people who interacted with his body, so medical doctors, chiropractors, X-ray technicians. If your child is in childcare and the provider might be changing your child's clothes, you'll want to warn them of any biological surprises they could find under those clothes.

How to tell the school

First, a quick reminder not to assume that you have to tell the school. Like with all other relationships and depending on your child's experience and expression of being transgender, some kids might opt not to need or want to come out at school. Some children and teens might also want to wait until the next grade or level of schooling. And some kids want and need to be affirmed immediately in their gender diversity. However, it's important to note that even though your child might wish the school to be informed and affirming, they are still allowed a certain level of privacy. Meaning, not everyone needs to know their prior name, how long they've been gender diverse, or any psychological or medical support they choose to receive.

There are three levels of oversight when it comes to being transgender in school. The first is from a school district level. You can look at the district policies for procedures regarding gender identities such as usage of desired names, dress codes, use of bathroom and changing facilities, and anti-bullying measures. If these policies are non-existent or not fulsome, you want to know before you meet with the school so that you know how much education and advocacy will be required on your part. Admittedly, it is much easier to talk with the school if you point out their existing policies.

The second tier of management is from the school administrative level, which is the leadership of your child's day-to-day experiences at school. We chose to disclose to the principal first when we enrolled in Mitchell's new school. At his old school, Mitchell told the Gay-Straight Alliance counsellor first, and I got called into the principal's office to explain what was going on. It was not a fun experience because I was not prepared. I had no idea what to ask for and how even to explain what Mitchell was going through. I would love to spare you such an experience. The principal sets the tone for the school, creates the culture of acceptance, and introduces further education for their staff to accommodate your trans kid. They are an important player in your child's safety and happiness.

The third level and much closer circle of relationship is the staff teachers. These are the people that your child interacts with the most. Teachers are the ones in the trenches. They also set the tone and culture in the classroom and create a sense of belonging. Teachers are the ones who lead by example with regards to misgendering or using your child's chosen name and other language that the students will emulate. They are the first to notice when your child is not being honored for who they are and if teasing occurs. In primary school, teachers can help by avoiding gendered phrases such as, "Listen up boys and girls," and they can avoid creating line-ups and teams of boys vs. girls. In high school, teachers have less intense contact and do less organization with the kids, but they can definitely shut down discriminatory talk when they witness it.

I have included some resources at the end of the book that help with knowing your child's rights within your school system. Also, here are some measures that the school can use to accommodate your child's transition either from a school level or that you would have to bring forward to the school district to include in their policies.

Preferred name changes can be done without going through a legal name change on your child's school record. Equally, all staff and fellow students can start using the appropriate pronouns. Permission can be granted to allow your child to use the proper bathroom and locker room or changeroom for their gender identity and a private space can be offered to non-binary kids. Note that there are cases where schools say that a binary transgender child could use the nurse's or staff's washroom, which is gender-neutral. However, that can be a way of singling out your child, which can cause as much anxiety as using the bathroom that doesn't align with their identity. Check with your child if they prefer one over the other.

Other topics you might want to discuss with the school are any areas of distress your child experiences. If they've been teased or harassed by certain people before coming out, you may want to make the school aware of this so staff can keep an eye out for worsening harassment from certain students. Talk to certain supportive peers ahead of time so that your child has an ally right away. That can be an older sibling or a very close friend who learns about your child's gender diversity before the rest of the class and school.

What about those who are less accepting?

While I was liberal-minded and championed human rights for many people, I wouldn't ever suggest that the transgender community occupied more than a passing thought in my mind before my son came out. I would not have identified myself as transphobic then, but knowing what I know now, I indeed said and did some transphobic things out of pure fear and ignorance after Mitchell came out to us. But my child, my dear beloved child, there was no way I could hate him, ever. Through the years of working with families of transgender kids, there have been innumerable times I have seen the staunchest, most conservative-minded, traditional, religious person completely embrace their trans child or grandchild specifically because it is hard to hate someone you unconditionally love.

That said, not everyone is ready to let go of their fixed mindset of whatever right and wrong conditioning they received in their lifetime. The temptation can be strong to try to win over someone and convince them that your dear child is not the monster they believe them to be, especially if this person is in one of the close intimacy circles. However, I have found that people fall along a Bell Curve of open-mindedness.

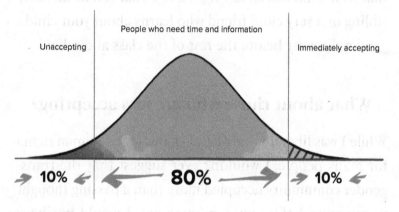

Bell Curve

Do you remember the Bell Curve they sometimes used to grade students? It can also be a depiction of normal probability in statistics. If you can visualize a bell shape on a graph, you can see a larger area under the curve in the middle than the two ends on either side. If you look at this curve from the point of view of acceptance, you will have 10% at one end who are completely accepting of your transgender child from the minute you disclose to them.

These are the people who champion you and help you in any way they can right out of the gate. Then you have 80% of people who need a little bit more time and information before they get it. Of that 80%, some are quicker to get to acceptance than others, depending on where they fall on the curve. Alas, the last 10% will not be accepting. Ever. And you honestly don't want to waste your time trying to win them over when there are people in the 80% who will require less of your emotional labor in getting their acceptance and support.

While this is a very overviewed exploration, the Bell Curve doesn't cover the devastating effect of having someone you love turn their back on you and your child. That emotional turmoil doesn't look like a nicely plotted graph; it looks like a dark, abstract mess. I hope that none of your closest circles of intimate relationships fall into that 10% of unaccepting individuals. Still, if they do, you must create healthy boundaries for your mental health and that of your child. Remember that what might seem like a minor slight adds up to torturous pain for the transgender person when compounded with the other barbs they receive elsewhere. It will help if you also protect yourself as the caregiver and primary support to your child.

Setting healthy boundaries with people who do not accept your child's identity can be easier said than done when it comes to certain relationships. Not everyone is someone you can choose to walk away from, especially if they are close family or if they and your child have a close established relationship. Allow me to walk you through the steps.

Establish what you will and will not allow. Of course, there are people who will require a little more time to understand gender diversity or who might make genuine mistakes with pronouns. But as a parent, you know when people are being mean, disrespectful, and unrelenting. Trust your gut if something feels intentionally hurtful. You may allow for more time for someone to process the shock or learn the new lingo, but you cannot allow someone to hurt your child. Be clear with yourself what behaviors and language are unacceptable around your child or in your own presence. For example, I won't tolerate someone constantly referring to my child as "used to be a girl" or using derogatory terms such as "tranny" or "he-she," and I will not allow anyone to send me books or articles that are meant to sow doubt about the validity of gender diversity. Finally, I do not allow people to use how "difficult it is for them to wrap their heads around this transgender thing" as an excuse for their language or behavior.

Be clear in your communication. Boundaries are not wishy-washy; they are firm statements that are not up for debate. No is a complete sentence. Say what you mean. Ask for what you need. Repeat yourself more than once. The last thing you want to do is open the door for people to start sending you unsubstantiated "evidence" around why they don't accept your child's gender diversity. You are not responsible for changing other people's mindsets or beliefs, but you are responsible for being clear about your boundaries and protecting your child's mental health.

Pay attention to your needs. While the most important factor here is to make sure that your child doesn't get hurt, the reality is that you also want to protect your emotional energy. Constantly playing the buffer with someone can get exhausting. You don't want to be so fried from negotiating with unwavering people that you have no reserves to help you child when they need a parent to lean on. Besides the fact that none of this happens in a vacuum—you still have the everyday frustrations of being an adult. Firm boundaries free up your energy to focus on your emotional needs.

Set your limits. The best advice I ever received from a therapist was to visit family who needed firm boundaries instead of having them over to my house, because it is easier to walk out than to ask someone to leave. Part of having a boundary is also to think ahead of what happens when someone crosses the line. Think of what consequences you can consistently follow through on and what impact they will have on you and your child. If someone refuses to understand or hear that what they are doing is hurtful and continues to hurt your child, set the boundary around if and when they can see your child at all.

This is not always an easy journey and it is a lifelong one. We never stop loving and caring for our kids. Of course, it gets way easier later, but those first few months and years are a slog, and the last thing you need to waste your energy on is trying to convert the unconvertable. Do not be ashamed to reach out to a therapist if you need help working through healthy boundaries with someone important in your life.

For the 80% of people dragging behind in their acceptance who fall a little more into the tolerance category, it can be just as challenging at times. Sure, they don't say outright that they dislike your child, but sometimes silence and cold shoulders are also hurtful. In the end, we all just want to belong and know that we matter. All of us. Every creed, race, religion, gender identity, social class, sexual orientation, ability, and age. Knowing that this is the main drive for people, imagine what it's like for someone to be told they're being tolerated.

You tolerate a rock in your shoe for a few steps until you can find a bench to sit down on and take it out. You tolerate a horrible smell in the public washroom because you have nowhere else to go and really have to go! You tolerate but turn your back to the bitterly cold wind as you leave the bus shelter and wait for the bus to stop.

Admittedly, tolerance is better than hate. But we're all hoping for more than to be tolerated, aren't we? Tolerating someone is not a heroic act of generosity. What they're saying is, "There is something wrong with you, but I will put up with it... I guess. You know, because I'm nice." It feels about as warm and fuzzy as, "I have no problem with what you do in private, just don't shove your existence in my face." Ouch.

When Mitchell came out as transgender, I had to check in with my own biases. I grew up in a very binary world. I had never heard the words transgender or non-binary until way into my adulthood. I had a lot to learn on this journey, but I strove to understand for the love for my child. We can bridge the gap between tolerance and support, but it does require some effort. It requires seeing the humanity in others. It requires asking questions and listening with an open mind to the answers without the hidden agenda to retort. It requires getting to know people that are different from the people in your immediate circle. And the most difficult part, it requires that you drop some of the right and wrong thinking that our current political and media climate is cultivating, which can undoubtedly be a challenge for the more tolerant and less accepting of your friends and relatives.

Support was not a linear overnight event for me; it may not have been immediate for you either, and I am not judging anyone who still needs to bridge the gap between tolerance and support as long as they are making the effort to bridge the gap and not looking for accolades for being tolerant.

You might read about TERFs (trans-exclusionary radical feminists) who are making a lot of noise about the number of pubescent girls who come out as trans boys. There's also a book out there that is getting a lot of attention on this same topic, suggesting that trans boys being affirmed is a trend, and it's an affront to girls. There is an excellent reason why more trans boys come out as transgender at puberty. Those who were assigned female at birth will have dramatic and drastic puberty. When people born with ovaries and uteruses start puberty, it is all at once. It is an undeniable and in-your-face opening into what society deems is womanhood. Menstruation can be very dysphoric to the trans boy, and that means that they need it dealt with much faster than the slower puberty experienced by trans kids who are assigned male at birth. That is one of the reasons why there are more trans boys in the system at puberty asking for medical intervention than trans girls.

However, there is another reason there are more trans boys and non-binary youth coming forward than trans girls, which has to do with misogyny. Our society accepts and reveres masculinity substantially more than femininity. As a society, we treat women as second-class citizens. We also treat effeminate gay men as second-class citizens and frown upon any femininity that men display. We have a very contentious relationship with femininity in women, as well. We judge women way more harshly than we judge men, and I'm sure I don't have to convince you of this. It is evident that men do have a higher place within our society, so of course, it would be much easier for a family to accept a boy into their family who was assigned female at birth than to have their son come forward and say that she is a girl.

A child who has been raised as a boy their whole life has been socialized and told repeatedly that everything about being feminine is wrong. They have to deal with that internally. They might be confident in their identity yet not want to express it until later in life when they have more reserves to face a prejudiced world.

When you disclose to people who are less than accepting that you are raising a transgender child, you might be sent "research" from these people to "help" you and your child. There are a few examples of trans adults who talk about regrets about medical interventions. These articles take the position that the adults changed their minds later on and feel like they were coerced into it or feel like the interventions happened too soon, and for that reason, they have regrets about "becoming transgender." These few articles are repeated over and over because there are so few of them. They are sensationalized and are meant to instill doubt.

Have you heard of the concept of confirmation bias? Confirmation bias means that we pay more attention to information that fits what we already believe about life and the world. Unfortunately, social media analytics are confirmation bias spreading like wildfire. We end up in echo chambers with people who espouse the same beliefs as us and often share questionable sources to confirm our bias on any topic.

Be careful of an idea that you have picked up online or that a family member may have told you about that says being transgender is wrong, affirming a child's gender diversity is wrong, or we should only affirm our children after the age of eighteen. If you go looking for that evidence, you will find it. Watch out for those rabbit holes because you will find evidence that is weak but has been manipulated to seem impressive.

When well-meaning friends bring these books and articles forward that negate your child's experience, say thank you and shut it down, because you don't need to have that confirmation bias. Being transgender has been scientifically studied for decades, and in many countries, this is not a new fad, and this is not an experiment being performed on your child.

Why allies matter

It is no secret that we live in divided times. No matter what topic comes up, there is usually a very stark delineation between good and evil, right and wrong, us and them. You see it everywhere from Apple or Android, to political parties. Sadly, you also see it within our transgender community. Unfortunately, some people feel that they are standing up for the oppressed when they shame our allies—those who genuinely try to learn about our community and empower it—for not being perfect enough.

I don't go along with the idea that minority groups like transgender people are powerless victims and cannot stand up for what they want. Your child doesn't need allies because they are poor, weak, and helpless. That said, we are still fighting for fundamental human rights in many places, and there is strength in numbers when it comes to voting at the ballot box or with our dollars as consumers.

We never want to be so ugly and mean that we alienate someone using the wrong terminology who wanted to support us. We also need to return to the beginner's mind every once in a while and realize that most of our terminology is "industry jargon" to a layperson.

I often hear from my friends, "I don't know what to say. I don't want to offend anyone." Most often, I heard this from friends and acquaintances who'd just found out that I have a transgender child and were struggling to use the proper terminology and not hurt anyone's feelings. When talking about Mitchell in his early childhood, they didn't know what pronouns to use or if they should refer to him as my son or daughter. I could tell that these people were trying. I could tell they were genuine. Today, I go out of my way to make it clear that before my son came out in 2016, I also didn't know what to say. I am only a few steps ahead on the path and happy to share what I know without making it sound like they are idiots for not knowing what AFAB stands for; instead, I patiently explain that it's Assigned Female At Birth, which is the most appropriate way to refer to my transgender son before we affirmed him as a boy.

This is something you can teach your closest friends or allies. Share with them that pronouns are tricky and can be a new concept to our older generations, but this is where you can make a huge difference in being a Super Ally—don't assume someone's gender by what they wear and how they style their hair. Instead, ask, "What are your pronouns?" BAM! It's that easy! And, don't be shocked if someone who presents as feminine or masculine asks to be referred to as they/them and identifies as non-binary.

It's also essential for us as parents and our allies to understand why some people are less generous than others when it comes to forgiving our ignorance and slip-ups. It may be your only mistake that day, but the person you inadvertently offended may have had that same thing said to them forty times before you uttered the words. Errors and microaggressions accumulate. That is why it's always great for you to practice new name and pronoun usage away from the kids and with your ally friends.

Also, people are all in a different place in terms of their coming out journey. Jody might be a super cool non-binary person who lets a misgendering roll off their back. At the same time, Amanda faces discrimination from her parents at home and financial insecurity while trying to find a job. The last thing she has energy for is explaining to a stranger the difference between transgender and transvestite. It's not easy for an ally to know who is in the best frame of mind to help educate others to be better allies. This is something, like pronouns, that you need to ask about upfront and be forgiving if it's not the best time to ask.

I share my journey with Mitchell with my heart on my sleeve to bring people closer, create a connection, and spread acceptance. I am far enough along not to be hurt or offended anymore, and it is not a huge emotional toll on me to teach and explain. Be gentle with yourself at first, because you may not be in that position of advocating just yet. You might still need to figure things out for yourself and keep your child safe and close. That's okay. Other allies and I are here to hold the fort.

Constantly coming out

Parents and caregivers get to take some of the pain away from our children by doing the emotional labor of telling certain people that our child is gender diverse. With their permission, of course. But this does become a chore for parents when we are also the ones who are answering questions, especially if we're not completely clear on the answers yet.

When Mitchell disclosed that he was transgender, I saw it as the proverbial coming out of the closet as the person he truly is and identifies as. For myself, what I needed was to go into my own closet. As I mentioned earlier, I slowly brought into my closet the people with whom I was comfortable sharing our experience. First, it was my two older children that I let into my closet along with my husband. Then, I added my best friends who lived across the country. I held them all close so that I had a safe place to talk about my feelings about Mitchell transitioning and how different our lives would be from what I had planned or imagined. We talked about the challenges of how I had to defend his right to be transgender with the principal, the dentist, and the music teacher, and about how all of the service providers that we interacted with who knew him as a girl had questions when he showed up as a boy.

For me, the social transition wasn't coming out of the closet. It was going into the closet and bringing in all of these people one by one who were safe so that I could make mistakes using the wrong pronouns and apologize and correct them, talk about my feelings, and get used to the fact that I had a transgender son. And then, at some point, you end up adding so many people into your closet as a parent that you also come out, or maybe more like bust out of an overfilled closet. You will be comfortable as the parent of a trans kid.

For some people, this happens within a week. They just know their kids so well, and they know that there's something up. Their kid comes out at a young enough age that they get it right away. It takes a little longer for others like me to gain the ease and comfort around the experience of raising a trans child. I was utterly supporting and affirming. I did everything that I was supposed to do on the outside of that closet, but on the inside, I struggled. This journey takes a little longer for some of us until we can come out and be champions and advocates for the transgender community. Now that I have become an ally, I am often the person invited into the parent's closet to help them process these new changes. My best advice is to give yourself some leeway. This may not happen overnight. It might take a little while, but you will find your place of comfort with raising a transgender child.

One of the most challenging parts about raising a trans-gender child is that I will never truly understand what it feels like to be transgender. I witness my son's journey, and I read all the information. Still, I identify as cisgender—with the gender I was assigned at birth—so I don't have the insider experience of what it's like to live as a gender you are not comfortable with and then dare to live authentically as the gender you know yourself to be. But that doesn't mean that I don't see the weight of societal expectations, and you know them too.

Gender as a social construct is one of the first expla-nations we all receive in the transgender community. The world is set up for us to make automatic assumptions about someone's sex categorization by the way they look, dress, speak, and act. Different cultures have different expecta-tions for men and women, but there are expectations in how either gender presents to the world. It's important to realize how much we are all conditioned to believe things without ever examining them. Can you know for sure that the clerk at your grocery store who presented as male was also assigned male at birth just by looking at them? No. And you also don't need to know that to have them ring through your milk and bread.

Genders carry certain expectations in today's society— even though we desperately try to advocate for feminism and equality. What do we ask women in their late thirties who just got married? "When are you going to have kids?" What do we ask men? "What do you do for a living?" These questions show that as a society we expect men to be providers and women to be mothers. While more women are choosing not to have children and men are choosing to be stay-at-home dads, that is not the initial assumption made by people around them.

The same can be said about our beliefs of what it is to be a mother, or a father or a caregiver. As mothers, we have an archetype that we are measured against. You know the one, I'll call it "the good mother." We are expected to be caring and patient and put our children first at all costs. We are supposed to be natural nurturers, teachers, nurses, and psychologists. For some cultures, this includes working full-time outside the home while being June Cleaver at home. Unfortunately, many of us judged our mothers for not reaching this pinnacle of perfection until we had children of our own and saw how impossible it was to be "the good mother." Still, way too many of us subconsciously carry these expectations of ourselves because we have also been conditioned to believe this is what a mother should be.

And so, we beat ourselves up as mothers of transgender kids for not knowing our child was transgender, for not being supportive enough fast enough, for having doubts and fears. Or we hold ourselves to this impossible standard of being "the good mother to a trans child" and twist ourselves into knots, putting our children first at all costs. I am not saying it is wrong to be a caring parent. I am asking how much of it is coming from a place of balance and care, and how much of it is coming from measuring up to what the world expects of you. You have every right to your emotions and processing. You are allowed to make mistakes. You are human too.

I often say a fish doesn't know it's swimming in water unless you take it out and it gasps for air. So do we as humans not know of our social constructs until they are pointed out to us. That said, we are operating in a world in which a majority of people not only blindly follow social constructs but also expect the same from those around them. Therefore, as a parent, you are going to feel like you are constantly being pulled out of the water or pulling others out of the water to bring them to a stark realization they don't want to face.

That is not always an easy space to occupy, and not all of us deal with confrontation the same way. But I am here to say that it does get easier. As parents, we eventually develop resiliency to coming out over and over. We find a way of naturally explaining our family to others and it flows off our tongue without hesitation. We develop an intuition around who is open to learning and who needs a boundary to respect our privacy. A wonderful side effect to watching our kids be brave and authentic is that we ourselves become inspired to be brave and authentic, and through practicing that bravery, we discover our authenticity. Raising a trans child is truly a gift.

You Time

I just touched upon some big topics around significant relationships in your life and your child's life. Let's slow things
down for a minute to center yourself. Take a deep breath.
Now pick up your journal again and ponder these questions.

1. What am I hearing underneath the variety of opinions
   being expressed on gender diversity?

2. What new connections or friendships am I making?

3. What are the boundaries that I need in place for
   myself?

4. What are the boundaries that my child is asking for that
   I need to help them uphold?

Chapter 4

❧

Social Transition

Between my experiences of working with people as a registered nurse, then raising four little ones, and then working as a life coach, I have come to know one fundamental truth about being human: we all want to be seen, heard, and understood. We want to belong and to know that we matter. That applies even more to marginalized people, including our transgender kids. Meeting this fundamental need of our children lies in affirming their gender identity. It's that simple and that complicated.

As I evolved while raising my four children, my parenting style focused on my kids' positive behaviors instead of the negative ones. At the time, I thought I was being avant-garde and using loving-kindness as my guiding principle instead of being authoritarian. Well, at least I tried. But I had no idea how painful it could be for my kids to be ignored for being who they truly were. This included my ignoring the signs that Mitchell was more comfortable displaying masculine characteristics. I thought that if I didn't see that he was a boy, I could "extinguish the behaviors" as if Mitchell's identity was like housetraining a puppy.

When we finally saw, heard, and understood Mitchell, when he came out at eleven years old, we ultimately affirmed his true self. We showed him that he belonged and mattered to our family. Then, we facilitated his social transition so that he could be seen and understood by the rest of the world. I believe this is where the mental health struggles that face the transgender community all originate. Affirmation. Can you imagine walking around in your life and having no one see you or acknowledge your existence? Can you imagine standing in front of a mirror and having nothing reflected back to you? Not belonging anywhere, not mattering to anyone? Now that you know why you want to help with a social transition, let's discuss how.

Pronouns

For my son Mitchell, transition meant going from female to male. He did not identify as non-binary. We had to use he and him pronouns after using she and her for eleven years. Yes, that was rough for us for a few months, as we made many mistakes. What helped was practicing with my husband and friends by using the proper pronouns even when Mitchell wasn't around. I would write he or him in texts. I would use he and him with my internal thoughts. Initially, we spelled his gender-neutral birth name in a masculine way and continued calling him by his birth name. While I thought I was lucky to be able to keep that part at least, I don't think it helped me mentally conceptualize my son as male. I will be covering name change in another chapter, but for now, know that it was much easier for me to use the correct pronouns once we had a new name for Mitchell.

Let's jump into the non-binary pronouns they and them. I am a writer, and I can certainly understand the grammar sticklers out there who believe that 'they' is a plural pronoun. But it isn't always, and it has never been strictly a plural pronoun. For example, if I am driving my car, and I witness a bike come by, sideswipe my car, and keep on going, I will say to my husband in the passenger seat, "Hey, that bike just hit my car, and they rode off! They didn't even stop to get my phone number for insurance or anything. How rude!" I will use they because I don't know if it was a he or her. After all, they had their helmet on and were dressed all in black. How am I supposed to see if they identify as a girl or a boy?

We can use they and them for an individual who uses those pronouns. Admittedly, it is tough for us older generations to start calling individuals they and them. I always admire how easily it rolls off the tongues of kids and teens. Again, we all need to practice, and it will come naturally to us one day.

The best way to address the mistakes we all make with pronouns is to apologize and correct yourself. That's it.

If you make a mistake and someone else corrects you, say thank you, make the correction, and move on. Don't make the apology a drawn-out dramatization of how horrible you feel about your mistake—describing that you're tired from a bad day, blaming your age, and on and on. You never want to force the person going through the transition, who is trying to assert their identity and struggling to make a place for who they are in the world, to have to console you because you feel bad for making a mistake. You would be putting your problems on the child, and you don't want to do that. Remember, the key here is to do what is most comfortable for your child, and the most affirming thing you can do is use the pronoun they ask you to use. That is the foundation of a social transition.

Clothes, hair and accessories

Even though today we live in an environment in which women can wear pants and men can be stay-at-home dads, and we allow our daughters to play with trucks and our sons to play with dolls, the reality is that our world is still very much defined by the two-sex binary. We are making progress as a society but not so much that we don't automatically assume that someone with long hair and a dress identifies as a girl. Our children have also been socialized in this world of males and females. Those who identify as transgender understand what is expected of the gender with which they identify. Also, our children are one of the first generations to understand the concept of non-binary—sometimes better than we do as adults!

Trans kids and teens know how they are most comfortable in expressing themselves. If your child identifies along the binary, they may want to affirm themselves with stereotypically masculine or feminine presentations. Because of how we are all socialized, and because they want to be seen and acknowledged as their gender, they might push the stereotypes we often try to avoid when raising our kids. For example, that might mean a whole lot of pink and glitter for trans girls. Often this means we need to buy them new clothes.

When Mitchell came out, we had to do a complete wardrobe overhaul. We had to change his bedding from pink and frilly to solid blue because it was clear that he wanted to express himself in his masculinity. We had to switch out his backpack, jacket, shoes, skates, and bathing suit. Depending on the age of your child, you might struggle to find clothes that fit properly. From the waist being too narrow or hips too broad, limbs too long or too short, off the rack shopping can be difficult. We managed this by finding a good tailor in our neighborhood, but there are online clothes suppliers that sell non-binary attire and clothes that work with a variety of bodies. Similarly, shoe shopping can be a challenge when looking for small men's shoes or large women's shoes. We've had luck when shopping the overstock and discount sections or online.

Cutting off his long curly blonde hair was one of the

steps that he took a few months before coming out to help make himself more comfortable. I had cried privately about seeing those curls on the floor in the hair salon, not knowing at the time how many tears I would shed for the changes about to come. And we cut his hair even shorter when he came out.

Change is not always easy, especially when it's not a change that we seek out. Supporting and affirming our children offers us many opportunities to face change and feel the resistance within ourselves. Some of us deal better with change than others. I happen to be the type of person who can roll with things pretty quickly. At least, I thought I was that type of person. The day I was folding the last load of laundry of Mitchell's old girl clothes to give away to donation, I cried again. Some of those tears were because I missed the girl I thought I would watch grow up. Some of those tears were from fear of the unknown, and to be completely honest, some of the tears were for the money I saw flying out of our bank account for having to replace almost everything Mitchell owned. Many of those things that I had bought with love and care were now discarded, donated, and sold on resell sites if we were lucky.

When we're talking about a social transition, social is right there in the name. It's not just within the four walls of your house. There is a social life attached to it. So you always have to check with your child and see what they prefer and what makes them comfortable. Some kids, young adults, and teens want to try on transitioning in the privacy of their room, or they want to do it within the household only. This might be a time of exploration and questioning, so do not be surprised if there is some waffling back and forth between their gender expression. That does not mean they are not "really" transgender. It is a matter of finding the presentation with which they are most aligned. Even people who fully identify with the gender they were assigned at birth sometimes switch up the level of masculinity or femininity in their style.

Tucking, binding and transgender gear

Sadly, not only is it expensive to change over an entire wardrobe from one gender to the other, the specialty garments for transgender people can also be quite costly. The money you end up spending also adds up if your child is still growing. But some pieces can be vital to your child's mental health if they are struggling with gender dysphoria. Some workarounds can be dangerous to your child's health. As a mother of four children, I fully understand the debate between buying what is necessary and what is nice to have, and some of these options are not frivolous but needed. It is also imperative that these pieces be sized appropriately. Because most of these items are mainly sold online, use the measurements guide every time you purchase them. These are not items that you can buy a bit bigger so your child can grow into them like we often do with shoes and winter coats. If you cannot afford to purchase these items new, exchange programs in certain cities and non-profit organizations will provide transgender gear at a discount or for free. Please see the resources section at the end of the book for some links. Now let's unpack all this gear, shall we?

Tucking is what we call hiding the bulge caused by genitals on transgender girls. This is done mainly to address the gender dysphoria that some transgender girls experience or to have a more feminine gender expression in tighter fitting clothes such as leggings. Tucking is achieved by pushing the testicles into the inguinal spaces from which the testicles descended at or after birth and then angling the scrotal skin and penis shaft backwards towards the butt. Once all those parts are squared away, trans girls then wear a pair of tight spandex underwear such as a bikini bottom or a gaff with panties over the top. A gaff is a supportive undergarment used specifically for tucking that can look a lot like a thong. Because gaffs can be expensive, especially if your child is still growing, some people make their gaff from the top part of a tube sock and the waistband cut out of an old pair of underwear. Please refer to the resources list for examples.

Next, we have chest binding for transgender boys. This isn't required until your trans son starts to develop breasts. Many non-binary people also wear a chest binder, and they are not used by only trans boys and men. Binders are essentially very tight undershirts that flatten the chest. It is essential to size the binder appropriately, not wear it longer than eight to ten hours, and never allow your child to sleep in their binder. Binders can cause back pain and constrict breathing if they are too tight or overused.

One of the first and most dramatic signs that my son was experiencing gender dysphoria was the day I found Mitchell taping his breasts with sheathing tape that was meant to be used for permanent seaming and sealing of joints in home construction. The red welts that appeared once he removed the tape were enough to convince him that this was not a permanent solution. The welts also convinced me that inflicting that much pain on himself meant this was something to take seriously. Note that there are many sites and videos out there teaching trans people how to wrap their chest in Tensor elastic bandages or use medical tape. The problem is that some children or teens might not do it properly or think that any tape can be substituted for medical tape and injure themselves.

Brands of medical tape that have been specifically developed for transgender people are widely available. The various tapes can be used on the chest for binding or on the genitals for tucking. Some people find taping more comfortable and less visible under particular articles of clothing. Things to consider when using tape are the expense of a disposable product, especially for tucking when replacing it after every visit to the toilet, and skin irritation and breakdown from the glue. I spoke with a top chest masculinization surgeon who doesn't recommend using tape. He said it can cause thickening of the skin long-term, which can cause elasticity issues that could affect surgery in the future.

Taping tends to be suggested as an option with bathing suits because of their snug fit. This can be avoided if girls wear a bathing suit with a skirt attached to it and boys wear a binder under a rash-guard swim shirt. In addition, some companies sell bathing suits specifically for transgender people.

A helpful product that has made an appearance on the market in recent years is period underwear, especially the sort that looks like boxer briefs. These offer menstruating transgender boys or non-binary teens the option of not having to deal with sanitary napkins or tampons, which don't always work with male underwear and can cause dysphoria merely from being handled. There are many different brand names on the market and online.

The final pieces of transgender gear to discuss are prosthetics—packers, which is the term used for male genitals, and breast forms. Silicone breast forms that you insert into a bra can be purchased online and in many lingerie stores specializing in prosthetics after breast cancer. You can also buy a silicone packer from transgender gear retailers, mainly online. Note that your child might need specific underwear or a packer harness or strap to hold it into place and prevent the prosthetic sliding down the leg of their pants. Similarly, a trans girl needs a bra to hold breast forms in place. All prosthetics should be washed regularly, and silicone can be boiled for sterilization before it is first used near genitals. Before you go out to buy costly prosthetics, there are also homemade versions you can make using rice in an old nylon stocking that you insert into a bra for trans girls or pin to the underwear for trans boys.

Social life

All things considered, Mitchell's social transition was pretty seamless because many of his interests had already been leaning towards the masculine side. The way he spoke, the way he carried himself, and the games he played all contributed to him appearing as, and often being assumed to be, a boy once he cut his hair, wore a chest binder, and dressed in boy clothes. For us, social transition included immediately telling our family, friends, and extended family one by one. Mitchell told the school before I got to do this. They changed his name and gender markers within the school system before I even spoke to them about it. He was doing extracurricular music lessons, so we talked to them about changing his pronouns and experienced no issues.

As mentioned earlier, this quickly became a social transition for the whole family because we were coming out as a family as Mitchell came out. Whenever I discussed him during that time of social change, I had to explain to people who once knew my daughter that he should now be referred to as my son. For the most part, this was also easy. Not to say that I wasn't a nervous wreck every time I had those conversations, not knowing who, out of the adults I spoke with, would negatively respond to my son and our family. But no one ever confronted me to my face or over the phone. There were a few acquaintances who dropped off our social scene, but they left quietly. The only negative sentiments I ever received were from keyboard warrior strangers online, and I easily choose to block that out of my life.

Kids and teens were also very accepting—for the most part. Mitchell did experience some drama when he first came out in grade six. Oddly enough, it centered on the students who attended the Gay-Straight Alliance with him. Mitchell was the youngest one in the group and the only transgender youth, whereas the other students identified as lesbian or bisexual. Looking back on it now, the whole incident seemed to be related to unrequited teen crushes and jealousy over who was dating whom and if that made someone a lesbian or not. Ultimately the middle-school drama culminated in an older boy punching Mitchell in the face for "dating" his friend. As I mentioned earlier, we pulled Mitchell from that school and have been extremely happy with the new school. Besides that episode, Mitchell has had friends of both genders accept him for who he is both at school and in other activities. After he came out, I also noticed a few friendships of Mitchell's quietly fall away, but that didn't seem to bother him. He joined a community-wide Gay-Straight Alliance in our city, run by our local Pride Society, and now has deep, enduring friendships with like-minded people.

All that being said, it can be very difficult as a parent to watch your child struggle through a loss of friendships. We must witness their grieving process and give them a safe space to feel those emotions. And when the time is right, you can encourage your kid to make new friends. But that is sometimes easier said than done if your child is socially anxious or hesitant because of their gender diversity. Here are some tips to help your child create authentic and healthy social connections.

Boost their confidence: You can boost your child's confidence when making new friends by affirming their gender and allowing them to feel good about their authentic self. If they are dressed the way that feels right and using the right name and pronoun, they will feel that much more comfortable in social settings.

Role play some conversation starters: Practice conversations with your child to help them feel more confident in new situations. Besides the role playing I have already written about in chapter two (see 'Rehearsal and safe spaces'), some things you can practice are asking to join in a conversation or game and texting a friend to ask them to hang out.

Enroll in extracurricular activities: Find an activity that your child enjoys and that will lead to being surrounded by other people who share that same interest. Sometimes, you have to think outside of the box of the usual ballet, baseball, or soccer and look for something that is less gendered and more unique, such as fencing or improv, for your child to find their community.

Host a get-together: Being in a large group can be intimidating for some kids. You can mitigate this by hosting a smaller gathering of one or two guests with an activity to keep everyone occupied. For example, you can host a round of minigolf or an afternoon of skating so there's opportunity to chat and connect but also an aim to the day.

Recruit teachers or coaches: You might want to connect with the other supervisory adults in your child's world who can help facilitate more socialization in your child's life. Maybe they can offer the suggestion of which friends seem to get along well with your kid, so you know who to approach for a play date or hang-out time.

Accept that your child might be introverted: Even though you might be concerned as a parent that your child would rather get lost in a book than hang out with friends at the park, that might just be part of what they enjoy. Some kids are happy with one or two close friends. I might sound like a broken record, but check in with your child and let them lead. If they are not concerned about the size of their social circle or how active they are with friends, you don't need to rush in and try to fix things.

The bathroom issue

If there is one topic that is very closely associated with transgender people, it is the conversation around bathrooms.

Trust me, I wish I could write a book about supporting your trans kid and not give this topic any ink, but it is still something we need to address. Public bathrooms have been gender-segregated for generations and uphold the world view that gender is binary. Women and men have also been socialized to use the bathroom in very different ways. For people who identify as girls or women, going to the toilet can be a social event. Women go in groups, talk to each other through the stalls, and make eye contact in the mirror as we wash our hands or touch up make-up. However, men and boys usually go alone and are in and out efficiently, with little to no chit-chat.

Though the narrative shared in the media centers on the fear of "a pedophile dressing as a woman" to access vulnerable girls in the washroom, the reality is that it is the transgender person who is most at risk. For example, gender misreading is an issue for trans boys because there is a violent intolerance of femininity in the men's room towards both trans men and gay men. Though the responses are not always as violent in a women's washroom, frantic calls to the police can be an issue for a trans woman or a non-binary person with masculine characteristics using a women's public washroom.

Sadly, not every public place has the option of a gender-neutral toilet. Often, we are stuck weighing up the safest option for our child while considering their level of dysphoria and distress while using the bathroom of the gender with which they don't identify. This also leads to a very real problem with dehydration among transgender people who fast and avoid drinking so they don't have to use the bathroom when they leave the house. As a parent, you might start to keep a mental inventory of places with gender-neutral bathrooms so that you can plan your errands accordingly and reassure your child they will be comfortable and can stay adequately hydrated.

Schools often try to accommodate gender-diverse children by offering them the nurse's bathroom or a staff toilet. This is a situation where you want to check on your child's comfort level. It can mean feeling singled out when all their other friends go to the bathroom together, or it can be a welcome relief not to have to face questions or comments from others. Another consideration is that boy's bathrooms are not equipped with disposal units for menstrual products. For some kids, menstruation is a trigger for gender dysphoria, and not using the bathroom of their choice can exacerbate those feelings. On the other hand, some non-binary kids are happy to push the boundaries of the status quo and petition their schools and places of employment to have menstrual products available in all bathrooms. It's always best to follow your child's lead, as they can tell you about their bathroom needs.

One last piece that might help alleviate some dysphoria for transgender boys is the ability to urinate standing up. I wrote about packers earlier in this chapter—prosthetics that create a bulge in underwear. Some trans boys also want the experience of standing at the urinal or when using the toilet at home. If that is the case, they would need a stand-to-pee (STP) device. Some are shaped like a packer and require the same harness or strap as a packer. Other devices are more funnel like and don't mimic the look of genitalia. Sadly, some of these devices have feminine names like GoGirl and Shewee, which might turn off a transgender male.

Sports

Every day, I thanked my lucky stars that none of my kids got so involved in sports that I was sitting in a freezing hockey rink at six o'clock in the morning every weekend, and I felt that way even before having to deal with gender diversity. Neither my husband nor I are competitive athletes, and our children followed our leads and enjoyed our cycling and hiking sports instead of competitive organized team sports. But I know this isn't the case for every family and that many of you are facing big decisions around participating in a sport, especially a gendered sport.

Much like public washrooms, sports are heavily gendered in team composition, who should compete against whom, and even the gendered presentation and practice within a particular sport. Although, as a society, we allow co-ed sports teams for younger kids when it comes to games like soccer, those also tend to be the games where no one keeps score and we're all just happy to have the kids running in the right direction. But once a game starts to feel a bit more competitive, we tend to separate boys and girls. Most people will attribute this to boys' more muscular body composition—though, in reality, that wouldn't apply until puberty is well established. Sometimes, there is also an undertone of keeping boys and girls apart because of a sexual implication of physical exertion and contact. Even in sports in which both boys and girls participate, such as figure skating, cheerleading, or dance, there is a gendered delineation of how one dresses and what moves are proper or fit the regulations.

So, as parents, how do you introduce gender identity into your child's beloved sport? This is a vast topic that pops up in the news regularly. However, it is important to note that despite some nasty rhetoric and attempts at creating transphobic laws, the Olympics recognize and allow transgender people to compete. If the highest international recognition of athleticism can open the doors for trans people in sports, there is hope for our kids playing minor league softball and lacrosse in the future.

Even though Mitchell wasn't in organized sports, we did have experience with some extracurricular activities that didn't match his gender identity. For example, he did not want to be part of Girl Guides, and you can probably guess why from the name itself. You might face the same with your child and their preferred sport—your trans daughter may not want to be on the boy's baseball team, and your trans son might want to be learning the rings in gymnastics instead of the ribbon routine. The issue will be convincing the sport organizers to accept your trans child into their organization as the gender they identify with and not what body part they have in their underwear. It might be easier to convince coaches of recreational teams to allow your child to participate than coaches of competitive teams. As with schools, there are different levels to sport organization—the local coach, the league, provincial or state level, and national boards. They all might have different rules and regulations to navigate.

But here's the good news. It is being done. Some brave trans kids are agitating the system in many sports worldwide, and they can be great examples of how to have your child transition within the sport they love. For instance, Quinn is a Canadian professional soccer player who is an excellent example of a non-binary person paving the way for our next generation of transgender athletes. They won gold at the 2021 Olympics in Tokyo and became the first trans athlete to ever win an Olympic medal.

Still, there is a genuine concern about a transgender child using a changeroom. Even if your kiddo is on a fabulous team and having fun playing or performing at their best, there's that uncomfortable piece about showering and changing clothes surrounded by people who don't have the same body parts. We experienced this as a family regarding sleep-away camp in other activities, and physical education and sports at school. There is no magic answer here besides asking for your child to be accommodated by offering them a private area to change and shower. Sometimes, that means your kid is changing in a bathroom stall. But it is not always unusual for shy kids to seclude themselves to change, regardless of their gender identity.

You Time

This chapter covered a whole lot of changes that are helpful to your child but might be a drastic change from your everyday experience. It's time to make sure you are filling your cup of self-care and goodness. Let's focus on you for a moment. Grab your journal, take a deep breath, and tackle these centering questions.

1. How do I express my gender? Is it always in a way that society would expect of me?

2. How do I typically deal with life changes? What is my healthiest coping tool?

3. How do I learn to accept changes that I can't control?

Chapter 5

∞

What's In a Name?

Name changes can be an emotional topic for many families. Some of us invested a ton of time and careful attention in choosing our children's names, perhaps for a whole pregnancy or possibly, like me, you had your children's names picked out in your preteens. Some names get passed down from one generation to the other, and they can have special significance in honoring a specific person or a special spiritual or cultural meaning. When a child says that this name you so carefully chose is dead to them, it can be a hard pill for a parent to swallow.

Another blow can come from the name your child chooses. I don't know if this happened to you, but while my husband and I were choosing the possible names for our unborn children, there was a long list of annoying co-workers, despised bosses, and former romantic partners whose names we refused to give our children. Some names just don't roll off the tongue quite right or a name just doesn't match your heritage. Then there are the names that sound silly with your last name. My husband's dad always pitched Peter Plunkett as a joke any time someone was pregnant in the family (sorry to anyone reading this named Peter Plunkett). We work just as hard deciding what not to call our kids as we do choosing their name. And all this only to have our transgender kid come to us eleven years later and want to be called a name on your no-go list! Then there are the non-traditional names that many gender-diverse kids and teens offer as their new name, such as Ace or Blade or Zelda, that might take some getting used to on our part.

When our son came out as our son, we started by changing the spelling of his birth name, which, when spelled differently, became a boy's name. I never loved it as a boy's name, but I felt it was convenient for all of us. And it was for us but not for Mitchell. His old name carried old memories. As easy as it was for us to use his new masculine spelling, we were still calling him the name we had called him as a girl in everyday usage. I had read up on the concept of the dead name and heard from others that using the dead name was a form of microaggression towards a trans person. When Mitchell asked to change his birth name—male spelling or not—we chose to affirm his experience and look for a new name that would suit him best.

Picking a new name

Depending on the age of your child, you might have some influence over the choice of their new name. It might feel odd to purchase or even request a baby name book from the library when your child is in grade school or high school, but that is a great place to start. Luckily, as an author who must name my fictional characters when I work on a piece of fiction, I already had a baby name book on my shelf when we were looking for a name for our son. I suggest you have a piece of paper next to you and jot down any names that jump out at you. Your child can have their list and so can any parent, caregiver, or sibling who might be participating. Then, it's a process of elimination to find the name that everyone likes or with which they can at least live.

But be prepared to have no input at all and have your child make the announcement one day. I have seen that happen a lot, especially with teens and young adults. Also, be prepared for possibly learning that your child has a name they have used for themselves in their mind for years, before even coming out to you and others.

When the new name doesn't stick

If your child says they want to change their new name to a different new name, you are not alone! Sometimes, kids and teens need to try on their new name for a while to see if it matches how they feel inside. Maybe they need something a little more gender-neutral than they first thought, or conversely, perhaps they need something a bit more feminine or masculine than the gender-neutral name they first chose. While I cannot jump on blaming gender diversity on peer pressure, I will say that I have seen situations where names are chosen with a group of friends, but after a few weeks or months, they don't sit so well.

As a parent, I know the hesitancy to be changing names repeatedly when a child wants to try a new one. I was concerned that it would make Mitchell's transition seem frivolous or that if he couldn't make up his mind over a name, how could we trust him to make up his mind about his gender identity? It can also be frustrating to finally start to get a new name to stick in our mind and stop making mistakes only to be given a new name to learn. I want you to know you are not alone with these thoughts and frustrations. But getting the name right is a massive part of affirming our kids. I promise that it does eventually work itself out, you will land on a name, and this small slice of time of uncertainty will be but a bump on the path. Since we know Mitchell is comfortable and happy with his name now and we have legally changed his name, we've told him any other name changes would be on him to do when he's an adult. We joke. Sort of.

Using the right name

The struggle to use the correct name is real. Just as real as the struggle to use the proper pronoun. The advice I offered for using a new pronoun applies here. You need to practice using the new name with friends and family at every chance that you get. When you make a mistake, apologize briefly or, better yet, say thank you for the correction and move on. Change your child's name everywhere you possibly can, with their permission, of course. Use the new name on your calendar, in texts and emails, and in your internal thoughts. Again, you will mess up. I messed up a lot. But it eventually stuck.

Pay attention to gendered nicknames too! In our home, the girls were sweetie, and the boys were buddy. I have heard terms such as princess, baby doll, missy, and young lady, and sport, mister man, slugger, pal, and dude, all of which have some gender-specific undertones in other homes. While it's been five years since we've used Mitchell's birth name, when my husband called the cat sweetie the other day, I felt the familiar pang of grief from not hearing him refer to Mitchell that way anymore. This wasn't a microaggression towards our child, just an echo from a past that we don't revisit much anymore. I feel the same tiny pang when I hear my child's birth name used by someone else in my everyday life, and you might too. We all have different eccentricities as parents of trans kids and feel more or less loss from each of the pieces that change on this journey. If the loss of the birth name or former nickname is one of those things that tugs at your heart, know you are not alone.

Changing names at school

This will be different in different jurisdictions, so you will want to look at the school district's policies and the school's rules around using a preferred name instead of the legal name on their school records. But know that even when preferred names are allowed, your child might still see their old name on official documents. This also varies from school to school, depending on what computer programs they use for attendance and grading. Some systems don't allow for having an official name and a preferred name, and in that case, it is up to the staff to remember to use your child's preferred name every day. Know they might make mistakes initially, the same way we parents make mistakes, and be sensitive to the accumulation of those mishaps throughout the day. They may not be purposefully aggressive, but the little things eventually pile up, and we welcome home a surly kid after school, wondering what we can do differently. Then there is the case of the substitute teacher who might not know to use the preferred name during roll call, which can be a huge issue for a child who is not out to the rest of the class.

ID anxiety

Social transition and using a new name with friends and family and at school can quickly become a new normal for your family, but some situations can easily disrupt that comfort. Our family lives with a tremendous amount of privilege, and we don't have to worry about our son getting carded by police as he goes about his daily life. However, that is a real possibility for many teens and young adults, and sadly even more so for Black people, Indigenous people and people of color. It can be terrifying to present as one gender and have your identification show a different gender, especially when faced with someone in authority whose ideological leanings you don't know. This is a real anxiety that we, as parents, may not consider when we send our kids out into the world. Or maybe you think about it and worry about it, as I did the first time we flew.

A few months after our son's social transition, we traveled across Canada as a family to attend a wedding. All his legal documents had his birth name and female as a gender marker, despite the fact that he very much presented as a boy to the airport security staff. I tried to put a brave face on for my son, but I was terrified that we'd be questioned every time I showed our tickets throughout the flights out and back. Two years later, we traveled for my dad's funeral. At that point, we had a legal name change, but his gender marker had not been changed. We were also travelling with testosterone and syringes, which upped my anxiety, as they could be another reason for security to stop and question us. I included with the medication a letter from Mitchell's psychiatrist that explained his diagnosis of gender dysphoria, which his doctor referred to as "walking papers" to use if he were ever stopped and questioned. Both trips went smoothly, and to this day, luckily, Mitchell hasn't had to produce his walking papers.

Note that we lived with this anxiety on a trip across Canada, where the law protects my child's human rights. However, there are many countries that we couldn't travel to, because in some places, gender identity is conflated with sexual orientation and being gay is illegal, and in some countries, it's punishable by death. Because laws constantly fluctuate between progress and regression depending on the government in power, even on local, provincial, and state levels in North America and Europe, my best advice is to always read up on where you plan to stay.

Even from an everyday-life perspective, consider all the places where your teen or young adult might visit without you and be required to present an identification card. In addition, you may want to investigate which of these places allow you to make changes without a legal name change, such as a library or a bus pass.

Legal name changes

First, how do you decide that now is the right time to make the change official? This is going to be a very personal

choice for your family. Sometimes, a trans child is very dysphoric about hearing their birth name and is in a situation
where that name invariably keeps coming up. Other times,
as was the case for me, it just becomes an annoyance to
explain why we call our child a different name than what
is on his official documents. I felt like it was outing him
continually, and it was also emotional labor for me to be
managing who needed to know what about my child. By the
time we made the legal name-change application, our son
had been out for about two-and-a-half years, he'd been on
hormone blockers, he'd been called Mitchell by the family
and everyone at school, and it felt right. For all of my love
and skill for writing, I abhor filling out government forms,
so I had been very slow to go from legal name change to
birth-certificate name change to gender-marker change.
And then, there's informing every other government and
insurance agency of those changes as well. Be forewarned
that some parts of this journey affect each of us differently.
I am much happier telling the world about my amazing son
and our journey here than filling out a form!

The process varies from state to state, province to province, and country to country. The resources section at the
end of the book includes some links to more information
for a few countries. In Canada, legal name changes consist
of filling in provincial government forms and paying the
fee. Different jurisdictions require either a commissioner of
oaths or a notary or lawyer to witness signatures, and some
require parental consent from all parents. Oh, and there

was also a criminal-record check, including fingerprints to make sure my boy wasn't avoiding criminal prosecution by changing his name. That was interesting.

We also have the option in Canada of changing the gender marker on our child's birth certificate, including X for non-binary individuals. There is a warning when choosing X as a gender that there are places that will not accept this gender designation. Interestingly, some parents are now opting for X on the birth certificate when their child is born, as more people recognize that gender is an identity and not always in alignment with sex. Mitchell was quite clear that he identifies as male, so we opted for the M on his birth certificate. The process was a bit more convoluted for us as we had to do his legal name change in the province in which we lived and then apply for his birth-certificate change in a different province. That meant more paperwork, more notarizations, more fees, and more waiting.

In the United States, the name-change practice is less governmental and more legal in process and requires a judge or magistrate to review your request. The method also differs according to the state in which you live. Some jurisdictions require you to post a name change in the newspaper, which removes all anonymity and can be devastating to someone trying to live their life stealthily in their new gender. I have heard of some parents bypassing this requirement in their state or county by pleading for an exception with the court.

Even though gender markers can be changed during

a legal name change in some provinces in Canada, other jurisdictions have different rules. As of the writing of this book, in the UK only people over the age of eighteen with gender dysphoria who have been living in their authentic gender for two years qualify for gender-marker changes. Please see the resources section for more information on legal-name and gender-marker changes.

Where to change the name

Once you have the legal name change done, you still have a few steps to complete. You now need to make sure that your child's name is changed. Everywhere. Here's a list of places to begin with, but it may not be exhaustive.

- Schools
- Extracurricular activities
- Day camps or summer camps
- Childcare providers
- The public library
- Museum or club memberships
- Department of Motor Vehicles (if they have a learner's permit)
- Public or school transportation
- Social Insurance Number
- Employer if they have a part-time job

- Banks
- Education Saving Plan investments
- Provincial/state or federal taxing authority
- Health insurance
- Other insurance agencies
- Passport office
- Child tax benefits

What happens to the old name?

Once you've been around the trans community long enough, you will hear the term "dead name" used to refer to the name you gave your child at birth. If your child is old enough, they may have already referred to their old name that way. Using such a negative and macabre title can be a bone of contention for many parents, who put so much effort into the name they chose for their child. Remember that a good part of the reason some children choose a new name is to get away from the life they had before transitioning and the trauma that came from living up to a gender that didn't match their identity. They may not have the same love for the name that you did.

Many people think that a dead name refers to the name being dead to the trans person. It actually comes from the era before transgender people could be out and affirmed in public, when it was illegal and dangerous to be transgender. Back then, when the trans person died, the name that would appear on their tombstone would be the name they had been given at birth which also became their dead name. It was the name that they would be known for after their death. It is a very morbid and sad backstory for this often-used term, but it is a remembrance of how in the very recent past, most trans people were unable to live whole lives, and when they were buried by their families, their preferred name would be lost to time and replaced by their dead name.

Because we are an affirming family, we do not use the term dead name in our home. I use birth name or old name. While we don't use his birth name, it's also not been made into something evil or threatening because, in reality, we will all meet other people throughout our lives who use that name—it's not Voldemort, after all.

And sometimes your child might be just fine with their birth name. However, they might choose to abbreviate it or change the spelling to make it gender-neutral. For example, some men are called Stacey, and some women are called Michael. If your child doesn't have a negative association with their birth name, they might keep it.

You Time

Let's turn the focus back to you and your feelings around potentially changing the name you once chose for your child. It's time to grab a cup of tea, maybe light a candle, and play some ambient music. Whatever helps you relax. Here are some questions for you to explore in your journal.

1. What would happen if I chose to let go of my child's old name and embraced the new one?

2. How can I create an empowering story around the new name?

3. How can I honor the old name with a goodbye ritual, even if it is alone and away from my child's awareness?

4. How do I typically cope with the stress of filling out paperwork, bureaucracy, and legal forms? Can I use support to get this done?

Chapter 6

❦

Do You Need a Therapist
or a Doctor?

From what I've heard from many parents over my lifetime, and know to be true myself, nothing is more painful for a parent than to watch your child suffer and be helpless to fix what is causing their pain. I can certainly attest to crying along with my babies when they were teething and with my teens when they experienced their first heartbreak. As parents, we suffer alongside our trans kids. We fear the pain of our child being singled out or victimized as a transgender person or the ever-present day-to-day sadness and anxiety so many kids live with while they struggle to affirm their true identity in the world.

Before you consider calling a doctor or a psychologist, looking to "fix" what ails your child, you want to take a breath and double-check if your child is experiencing any distress or if it's all your own. We live in a fast-moving society that is set up to offer the instant gratification of the quick fix. You can order almost anything online and have it delivered to your home the same day or the next day, and that has conditioned us to be impatient with the many human processes that take time. You have to get comfortable with being uncomfortable. Not knowing if your child will be okay, if they are going to be bullied, if their body will betray them, all of that is uncomfortable. And none of it can be fixed with an overnight delivery or the click of an app.

I want to reiterate the difference between exploring gender expression and gender dysphoria. A transgender child who only explores their gender expression and has no body distress doesn't need to be rushed to a counsellor. They will need to see a therapist under the same conditions as any other child: if they feel anxiety, sadness, helplessness, or hopelessness that interfere with daily living activities and lasts as long as many days to weeks, or if there is a learning issue and neurodivergence. Remember, being transgender is not a mental illness. However, sometimes children need a gender-diversity-informed therapist to help them work through an exploratory phase or when dealing with someone important in their life who isn't quite accepting or affirming transgender kids, teens, and young adults.

A transgender child will not need to be seen by a doctor for transgender healthcare until they start approaching puberty. Until then, regular check-ups and medical care

are the same as with any other child. However, you will want to let the doctor know about your child's body parts not matching their gender so that they can assess the health of those body parts as needed. I suggest you have a phone call with the doctor beforehand, without your child present, to prepare them and so that they can be sensitive to your child's needs during the medical appointment. Also, you'll want to be assured that your doctor is affirming gender diversity, which can be done on that same phone call.

When you do need professional help

Now that I just wrote that children don't automatically need to see the doctor or a psychologist when they come out as transgender, I will admit to immediately booking those appointments. But, in my defense, I knew very little about what it meant to be transgender and what I did know was from my days as a registered nurse a good decade before Mitchell came out. When I studied psychology during my nursing training, being transgender was considered a mental illness. The term they used in the Diagnostic and Statistical Manual of Mental Disorders back then was "gender identity disorder." So, when my child said he was transgender, my first thought was that he needed a psychologist, stat.

As I will get into in the next chapter, Mitchell dealt with some mental health struggles before he came out as transgender. Going to the psychologist for help wasn't out of step for our family. In fact, in hindsight, what we thought were behavioral issues, mild depression, and social anxiety could all be chalked up to dysphoria. My mother's intuition said it was time to get the professionals involved. I turned to Google. Where else did one turn for answers in 2016? A search for "LGBT therapists in Calgary" brought up a list of names, so I poked around a few websites and narrowed in on the one that seemed solely devoted to LGBTQIA+ clientele. Then I made an appointment with our family doctor, knowing that I needed a prescription for the therapist to be covered by our extended health plan.

On the day of our appointment with our family doctor, my child was anxious, but in a good way. He felt what I later learned was gender euphoria from having his gender identity taken seriously. Once we'd been seen by our general practitioner, Mitchell and I were at opposite poles of anxiety as I dealt with my apprehension boring a hole in my stomach. I'd spent a lot of time in the presence of doctors as a nurse. I knew how difficult it was to have a patient expect answers when the doctor didn't have any. Dr. Rasley looked at us both with absolute compassion and said, "I have never had a transgender patient. I don't know what to do." I was grateful for her honesty.

Initially, only my husband and I met with the psychologist. She wanted to get to know our child through us first and assess the situation. So we poured out our concerns of the last two years. Everything that went right before that. Everything that had changed. Our child's lifelong battle with anxiety. The recent flirting with isolation and depression. The bullying. All our theories about why we thought she would want to be a boy suddenly. About halfway through, I was honest about the signs I didn't want to admit to myself—that she had been a tomboy for the better part of four years and that her period was a huge stressor and not just in the PMS kind of way. After a lull in my monologue, the psychologist countered with the steps we needed to avoid hurting our child.

When the therapist spoke, she used male pronouns when referring to our kid. It took me a few minutes to clue in to who she was talking about. She explained that parents of transgender kids typically chose to move forward in one of three ways. You can completely embrace your child's view of himself and support his transition medically immediately at eleven years old, completely deny his thoughts and feelings and refuse to accept transitioning, or fall somewhere in between—not deny your child's feelings, start using male pronouns, and allow him to socially transition without starting any medical interventions. I knew that completely shutting down the whole idea of transitioning was not something with which I could live. I could already see a difference in our child when we affirmed him. I was quite happy with the middle-of-the-road option of social transition. I had not yet arrived at the idea of medical intervention. It had only been a few months since learning this news about the daughter I thought I'd been raising.

Finally, the therapist gave us the information we needed

to be added to our local children's hospital's gender-clinic waitlist. Because the waitlist was two-and-a-half years long, she suggested we ask our family doctor to put in a referral as soon as possible. That would also allow us time to live within the social transition world for a while.

Please note that all of this happened away from the eyes and ears of our child. It was invaluable for us to gather this information from a professional with first-hand experience of transgender children. After that appointment, Mitchell saw this particular therapist for only a few sessions. He was so happy to be affirmed by her that I assumed all was well and he didn't need counselling. However, a few months later, thanks to social issues at school that I discuss in the next chapter, we explored psychotherapy once again.

One last note on a reason an older child might want to speak with an affirming therapist. Depending on your child's age and the environment in which they were raised, there can be internalized messages heard over a lifetime through socialization that there's something wrong with being transgender. They may have been internally dealing with their deep-seated knowledge that their identity doesn't match what the outside world expects from them, but at the same time, be dealing with living in a world where transgender people have until very recently been underrepresented or a community and faith in which being transgender is considered wrong and, possibly, evil. Those incongruent internal and external realities can cause the trans person much grief and distress, and they might want to unpack that with a trusted and affirming professional. Just because a person is transgender doesn't mean that they, too, can't be lugging around some transphobic baggage from their upbringing. That baggage needs to be professionally unpacked to help with self-worth and self-acceptance, and sometimes that work has to be done before the trans person is ready to be out and proud and loud.

Finding the right care

If your child identifies as non-binary or the opposite gender to the one they were assigned at birth before they reach puberty and they are experiencing gender dysphoria, it is time to consider transgender healthcare. There is medical advice available, and the World Professional Association for Transgender Health's (www.wpath.org) established international standards guide the healthcare team on if your child would benefit from puberty blockers. These are reversible, allowing your family and the medical team to decide if cross hormones will be needed. It's important to note that if your child identifies as non-binary, you can only suppress puberty for so long, and they will need to choose which hormones to deal with as an adult. Hormones are an essential factor in the health of the human body beyond reproduction purposes. They protect bone and heart health and prevent certain cancers.

In Canada, gender-affirming medical care is covered by our universal healthcare system. Because healthcare is a provincial jurisdiction, wait times can vary depending on where you live and if the clinics are well-staffed and well-funded. Most clinics require a referral from a family doctor, but some are now accepting referrals from mental health professionals. I am told that there is a similar process in other countries. The main issue in getting access to gender-affirming medical care seems to lie in how far away you live from your closest clinic.

The other main factor in accessing affirmative care for your child depends on the government elected to your local legislative body. Unfortunately, extreme social conservative governments are attempting to outlaw many protections for transgender youth. Though human-rights activists are battling these restrictions in courts, in the meantime, doctors are not practicing affirming care, and gender clinics are not popping up in, say, conservative rural areas. This is a real and present concern for many families of trans kids. Short of moving, you might be able to find care through telehealth options and video conferencing, especially for mental health support. Unfortunately, these may not all be covered by health-insurance plans. Be sure to qualify all practitioners before engaging them.

Questions to determine if your care provider is affirming

1. Does your office have a gender-identity and gender-diversity policy?

2. Are your staff trained to be sensitive to gender diversity?

3. Do your forms offer more than male or female as options, and does your records system allow for changes in pronouns, names, and gender markers?

4. Do you have other transgender or gender non-conforming clients?

Family therapy and parental therapy

Sometimes, kids are just fine with their gender expression and not concerned with their body, but as a mom or dad or caregiver, you are struggling to come to terms with raising your child in a different gender than what the doctor exclaimed when she put that baby in your arms for the first time. This is your full-fledged permission slip to seek professional help to deal with the massive upheaval in your family composition. There is no shame in needing to work through the long list of emotions we covered in chapter one. I know very well how much we, as parents, put our child's care and wellbeing ahead of our own and focus on making sure they are okay. You might feel that if your child is happy and adjusting well with their gender diversity, you should be happy too. Please do not feel guilty for seeking help when your child doesn't need it. Look at it as the old "put your oxygen mask on first" idea. Your child might be fine without therapy right now, but the sooner your needs are met, the sooner you can be an even better support to your child if and when they do face challenges.

Then there is the possible need for family therapy if the disclosure of your child's gender diversity is causing friction within the family relationships. Sometimes, we need a neutral third-party mediator of sorts to help navigate everyone's feelings and emotions. While we didn't have to deal with any huge dissent from other family members when Mitchell came out, my husband and I processed the news in different ways and at different paces. Having someone tell us that all of our reactions and inner thoughts were valid helped our marriage immensely.

Here, again, you want to make sure that the person you are hiring affirms the transgender community. Many parents seek out therapists and counsellors who are transgender themselves or have trans family members and real-life experience. That is nice to have but by no means a necessity. A well-trained licensed professional who affirms and supports or, better yet, advocates for the transgender community will be a great ally to your family.

Therapeutic add-ons

As with many things on this journey of raising a transgender child, not everything exists on a binary of you need a doctor and psychologist or you don't. There are other options for the in-between stages. One of those options is to find a local support group where you can connect with a community and feel a little less alone.

In chapter two, I wrote about a peer-led support group that I have co-facilitated for the past four years. Before creating that resource for our city, my husband and I drove to another city to attend a support group. It was a group that met once a month, was led by a social worker, and specifically served parents and caregivers of gender-creative kids under fourteen. As a bonus, there was on-site childcare, which meant that our kids also got to interact with other kids just like them.

Both my husband and I found this group invaluable. Meeting those other parents and hearing their stories brought a stark reality to something that, up until then, was a mere concept in our mind. My husband often recounts how before attending that first meeting, he held on to the hope that because Mitchell came out to us at eleven instead of when he was a toddler, there might be a chance that this was all a mistake. But when we met all the other families whose children asserted their true gender identity at various ages, including the same age as our child, he felt less uncertainty and more resolve to support our boy.

So many of them grappled with the same questions and emotions we faced, and we were grateful for a safe space to ask questions and share our feelings. After almost a year of attending that group, I knew that we needed the same thing in our city, and when I couldn't find it, I created it.

I found other practices extremely helpful to keep me grounded and balanced, and I shared a few of them with Mitchell, as well. My absolute favorite is to get out into nature. We happen to live close to the Canadian Rocky Mountains, so nature involved hikes on mountain trails, usually to a waterfall or lake. I often see and feel an enormous release of tension from everyone in the family on these hikes. It's like a mini vacation from the world's expectations where we all get to be in the present moment precisely as ourselves. On the days when I can't escape to the mountains, I walk the dog near our home, and other times, I stand on my front lawn in my bare feet.

Something else that I find helpful is to listen to guided meditations on YouTube or phone apps. I personally like something where a person guides me through relaxation, because when there were so many anxiety-filled thoughts rushing through my mind, I couldn't imagine clearing my mind completely. I also learned to use the Emotional Freedom Technique, or tapping, from some free YouTube videos, and they helped calm my mind and body. I shared those with Mitchell at the very beginning when he suffered from panic attacks.

None of these add-ons are meant to replace professional

help when warranted, but they can be inexpensive comple-
ments. Anything that builds our resilience and creates calm
and connection is a good idea, in my view.

Why not wait until they're adults?

After Mitchell came out, but before I went public with what
was going on behind closed doors in our family, I brought
up the topic of trans kids with a good friend who also
happened to be a loud and proud lesbian. As a member of
the LGBTQIA+ community, I thought she might have some
insight on how to proceed. I was shocked by her response,
"No child should be allowed to be transgender. Nothing
should ever be done before the age of eighteen." She was
pretty adamant about her stance. I had heard it before
from others, and you will find many socially conservative
lawmakers singing the same tune. But too often, these are
opinions that have been formed without all the facts.

It is also important to note that some medical professionals and counselling professionals believe that transgender
kids should not exist. They believe that transgender people
should only ever be affirmed in their gender identity over
the age of majority, whatever that number might be in their
jurisdiction. Those are the professionals you want to avoid.

There is a cost to waiting until your child is the age of
majority to initiate any medical or even social affirmation of
their gender diversity. Besides the statistics around suicide
attempts and the higher incidence of homelessness in trans

teens, here's what happens when you wait until adulthood to affirm your child's gender. First, they will internalize that there is something wrong with them instead of being affirmed for who they truly are and with the full opportunity to play around with what gender means to them.

They will also miss out on the opportunity of exploring gender while on puberty blockers. I will be going into a bit more detail on this medical option in the last chapter of the book, but for now, just know that puberty blockers prevent the development of secondary sex characteristics. That means that if you wait until your transgender daughter is eighteen to allow her to explore being transgender, she will have developed a beard, will have had her voice drop, will have had an Adam's apple develop, and will have longer arms, longer legs, wider shoulders, and smaller hips, which is what happens to a teen who is assigned male at birth as they go through male puberty. If you wait until your trans son is eighteen to allow him to explore his gender identity, he will have developed breasts, have developed wider hips, and have been menstruating for all of those years. In both situations, those physical characteristics will make it more difficult for them to fit in with their peers. In addition, it is more difficult to cover up those physical characteristics as they express themselves as a different gender.

Waiting until your child is eighteen before addressing the physical aspects of being transgender means that you are adding extra surgeries and more cosmetic procedures, such as laser hair removal, later on that you could avoid if you addressed things sooner. Not to mention the extra stress and mental load on your child in the lead up to turning eighteen. Essentially, by not wanting to address it before then, you are saying that only adults can be trans, yet everyone is assigned a gender and expected to express a gender from birth.

When we say that we cannot trust a child to know what is right and wrong with their body, we enter a gray area around consent. As a society, we spend way too much time taking consent away from children, which is very dangerous. There is much talk about the fear that the transgender community is somehow associated with pedophilia, such as the fear that transgender women are just men who want to have access to young girls in locker rooms and bathrooms, but in reality, if we deny the existence of transgender children we are saying that children cannot fully consent to their identity. *We are removing the ability for children to say no to something that feels uncomfortable with their bodies.*

Therapy to avoid

Another consideration for parents who are seeking care for their children is the existence of reparative therapy or conversion therapy. Conversion therapy is dangerous to our trans kids, yet it is sold as a fix. It is positioned as a solution that will return your life to "normal," and that can be seductive to us parents who are afraid for our child's mental health, physical health, and future. You don't want to endanger your child by allowing such therapy to be performed on them, but it is not presented as dangerous. It is presented as offering comfort in a whole world of uncertainty and won't have the label "conversion therapy" on the brochure. Conversion therapy can come in many forms, such as neural repatterning or spiritual cleansing. The biggest issue with these therapies is that they teach your child that there is something inherently wrong with their identity. You will want to steer clear of any medical or mental health professional, coach, clergy, or counsellor whose goal is to remove from your child the concept or idea that they are transgender.

You Time

As parents and caregivers, we carry a huge responsibility to make sure our kids are safe, healthy, and happy. That's completely expected. But in order to be effective in our care for our children, we need to care for ourselves. It's time to find a quiet place to be with your thoughts and your journal.

1. How comfortable am I with the idea of therapy and counselling?

2. What are my views on body ownership and consent?

3. What has worked best for me in the past to stay grounded and find balance?

Chapter 7

◦~∞~◦

When There's More Going On

Long before my son Mitchell came out as transgender, both his dad and I had concerns about our then daughter's mental health. She seemingly went from a sweet, eager-to-please, studious, and kind child to an equally sad and angry kid. I remember vividly the days I sent her to school in tears. At the time, with the information we had, I thought her girlfriends were being mean to her and excluding her from playing with them. She opted to play with the boys instead. But this was in grade four, when the lines of 'girls play with girls' and 'boys play with boys' started to be more defined. Then the disagreements began to escalate. While the girls decided to bicker and use cutting words to hurt each other, my child lashed out physically, much like how boys react when confronted. To the staff and administration, and us as parents, it was perfectly okay for her male classmates to bodycheck each other into a brick wall as they played roughly and for girls to say horribly mean things to each other. Still, it was not okay for our child, who presented as a girl, to push another girl during an argument. Of course, I didn't know then that my child was behaving in alignment with his gender identity.

Those school incidents were little traumas that eventually cumulated in our ten-year-old becoming even more depressed and socially withdrawn. Finally, we brought her to a psychologist who did some testing and diagnosed generalized anxiety for the panic attacks we had been dealing with during storms and fire drills. But the label didn't change anything, and her behavior continued to be disruptive at school.

I was concerned that our kid was living down to the label of "the problem child" in her class, and I had hoped that moving across the country would give our child a fresh new start. But within a few months of starting at the new school, she started getting into trouble again for what I can best describe as not following the social norms expected for a ten-year-old girl. She continued to isolate herself and have panic attacks. She continued to not fit in with her girlfriends. And then, two months after turning eleven, Mitchell came out to us as transgender. As mentioned earlier, my first reaction was to book an appointment with a psychologist.

What I didn't know then, in the way I understand it now,

was that being transgender was not a mental illness for my child. However, the trauma Mitchell experienced while trying to conform to all of society's rules for the role of being a girl caused him to feel depressed and anxious—to the point where he battled with suicidal thoughts.

Depending on the study and the country and the wording, you can find a wide range of statistics that show a considerable increase in suicide risk among transgender youth compared to the general youth population. I have seen statistics reporting that 41–64% of trans youth consider or attempt suicide compared to the 4–12% average for all youth (The Trevor Project 2021; Taylor *et al.* 2020; Bauer *et al.* 2015; Olson *et al.* 2016; Garriguet 2021). Fear of their child attempting suicide will turn the most transphobic parent into an imperfect supporter if only to keep their child alive. If you feel that your child is at risk of hurting themselves, I am begging you to find them the affirming professional support they need.

I was naïve to how much of a psychological burden my child dealt with from the age he began to carry the weight of trying to fit in as a girl and then later the significance of expressing himself as a boy for the first time. I didn't realize that saying, "I'm transgender," wasn't some magic cure to the trauma and mental load Mitchell was bearing. His suicidal thoughts culminated in an awkward attempt at school six months after he came out and we affirmed his masculinity. When I think back about the incident now, I picture a little fawn trying to stand for the first time, desperately trying to gain his footing surrounded by unforgiving middle schoolers who had such ingrained expectations of what it meant to be male or female and straight or gay. They gave him no room to learn to stand and walk.

My mind froze in absolute pain and terror when I received the phone call from the school asking me to pick up my child and bring him to the hospital for a suicide attempt. I don't wish that phone call on anyone. I don't remember the drive. I remember desperately trying to hold myself together as every fiber of my being threatened to unravel while I explained to the triage nurse why we came to the emergency room. My child needed help. Deep down inside, I also needed help to make it through one of the scariest days of my life. But for the time being, the priority had to be keeping my child alive and holding on to the hope that they could return him to that happy kid I hadn't seen in years.

That ER visit turned into a fast track on the waitlist with the gender clinic at the children's hospital, which had a substantial positive impact on Mitchell's mental health in the long run. But I don't want to minimize how awful it was for Mitchell from the time he started menstruating until the time he stopped menstruating nor the impact gender dysphoria has on a whole family when a child is desperate for help.

Signs that something is up

It can be difficult, as a parent, to pull apart typical child and teen behavior of pushing boundaries and exerting their independence from mental health struggles from gender dysphoria. I know that as a teen, I lived in my room, so it was difficult for me to tell if Mitchell's social isolation was typical or an indication that his mental health was affected.

You should never diagnose your child from something you read in a book or online; do see a professional if you are concerned about your child's mood or behaviors. And do follow those gut feelings that something is up. Here are some signs that we saw in Mitchell that helped us know something was amiss. Mitchell went from being told he should be tested for giftedness to a dramatic drop in his grades. He also dropped certain activities that he used to love, or he barely participated in them when we forced him to attend. He wouldn't talk about the future and couldn't imagine what he wanted to be when he grew up. Mitchell did not self-mutilate, but I know some of his friends would cut themselves when they were at their lowest. And at his lowest, Mitchell said out loud that he couldn't go on and battled suicidal thoughts. If your child or someone you know is dealing with difficult emotions around their gender diversity, you can find the crisis hotline number for your country at www.translifeline.org, or https://switchboard.lgbt and www.mindinsomerset.org.uk in the UK.

The correlation between mental health issues and being transgender

Let's start with a bit of a rundown of what I mean when I use the word correlation because there can be some confusion and fear around mental health. As a mom, I bring all this up because I would confuse the correlation between mental health issues and being transgender with cause and effect. Unfortunately, I also see many people in support groups for parents of trans kids automatically associate mental health struggles with being transgender as though their child will forever be suicidal or suffer from social anxiety.

Here are three words that can often get jumbled, especially if we read clickbait blog headlines or social media posts instead of scientific journals—concurrence, correlation, and causation. Concurrence is when two conditions occur simultaneously, such as the sun shines and it is warm outside. But is it always warm out when the sun shines? Not in the dead of winter in northern Canada, I can assure you. For example, your child can identify as non-binary and also be diagnosed with multiple sclerosis. One doesn't cause the other; not all non-binary kids have multiple sclerosis, and not all people who have multiple sclerosis are non-binary.

Correlation is when one condition is associated with the other and they tend to be observed at the same time. For example, I tend to feel hot when the summer sun is shining on me. I could also be suffering from a perimenopausal hot flash or a fever, but for the most part, I get warm on sunny summer days—these two things tend to happen together. An example of this would be that a child who is not being affirmed in their gender identity and is teased about their appearance at school might also suffer from hopelessness and suicidal thoughts. Of course, there could be another explanation for why these things seem to happen together, like if I had a fever when I felt hot mid-summer, but for the most part, they're related.

Finally, causation is one condition having a much more direct effect on the other. My red, sore, peeling sunburn on my shoulders after an afternoon outside in the summer with no sunscreen is caused by the sun. We don't know why our kids are gender diverse. Some theories are floating around regarding brain structure differences and in utero hormone levels, but the studies have not been conclusive. To be honest, I hope they never do find causation because I wouldn't want people to try to reverse or prevent it. As much as I struggled with Mitchell coming out when he was younger, and as much as he struggled while we were all learning to affirm him, it was worth it to have this exceptionally amazing child today. I wouldn't change a thing.

All of that to say: there is a correlation between mental health struggles and being a transgender child, teen, and young adult, in some people, but not all of them. For the most part, once your child is affirmed and living their life in the expression they align with most, mental health struggles ease to the rate of the general population. This doesn't mean that all affirmed trans kids never suffer from mental health disorders; it means they do so at the same rate as everyone else.

According to the Canadian Mental Health Association, some of the mental health challenges that are correlated to gender diversity are depression, anxiety, obsessive-compulsive and phobic disorders, suicidality, self-harm, substance use, and post-traumatic stress disorder (PTSD).

Gender diversity and trauma

There is some great work being done in the realm of trauma awareness, and as such, many disciplines are now looking at a trauma-informed approach to their practices. I often hear about the trauma that transgender people experience just by living in a world that "others" them, but I was curious how my trauma and my triggers and responses affected my transgender son after he came out to me.

I experienced many adverse childhood events, from my parents divorcing when I was five years old to the unsettling nature of moving every year. Both my biological parents were alcoholics, and my mother's second of four husbands abused me. I experienced abandonment and neglect but learned very early to be a responsible child and keep up appearances. Unfortunately, that habit stuck around well into adulthood and showed up as perfectionism, needing to be in control, hyper-independence, and the need to stay busy.

When I look back at my responses to Mitchell coming

forward at eleven years old, an age when I lived through the worst of my trauma, I can be confident that much of what I said and did was from a place of reactivity. I was a wounded child again, trying to be the responsible adult, and way too concerned about maintaining control, caring what other people thought of me and my parenting skills, and wanting to hide what I then labeled as a shameful secret. My saving grace was that I had done a considerable amount of healing by the time Mitchell came out. So while I was initially operating from a trauma response, it was short-lived and addressed in therapy.

However, I know that not everyone reading this book is a childhood sexual abuse survivor or a refugee from a war-torn country. Trauma is relative and doesn't have to be something that would make the nightly news. Sometimes, it is felt by a child as emotional neglect. Sometimes, it is attachment issues because of their parent's own trauma, addictions, or alcoholism. This can be easily discounted by saying that your dad went to work, and he was a functioning alcoholic, but the true impact of when a parent is abusing substances is that they are detached from emotion; therefore, they can't truly show up for us in that state. That is childhood emotional neglect. Trauma can be bullying that you experienced in grade school, body shaming from friends and family, an accident, growing up in poverty, a parent suffering from a mental illness, divorce, foster care and adoption, the death of a loved one, witnessing abuse or an accident, and other strong emotional situations.

The ways these traumatic events show up in our lives as adults are varied—from anxiety, to avoidance, in addition to the behavior I displayed myself such as busyness, fierce independence, wanting to control situations and people, trying to make one's child's childhood better, perfectionism, and fear of what people think of us. Our child going through something at the same age that we were traumatized as kids can trigger our traumatic response.

Traumatized parents might experience enmeshment with their children. Enmeshment could look like having no real boundaries with your child. This shows up if you feel your child's emotions as if they were your own or they are your best friend. This will often show up as an over-involvement in your child's life and hinder the development of their independence and ability to make their own choices. When a parent's identity is completely intertwined with their child, such as a "dance mom" or "mother of the bride," they live for the story they told themselves about how their child's life would be. As the parent of a transgender child, that can throw us completely off course.

Finally, for those of us who experienced abandonment issues and then nurtured what I like to call the "disease to please" in order to never have anyone leave us again, raising a transgender child can awaken that abandonment wound. Especially if there are people in our circle of friends or family who are intolerant of gender diversity. This can be a painful contortion of trying to appease everyone while protecting and honoring your child.

There is no easy solution to dealing with trauma and definitely not something I can suggest flippantly in a book. But I want to acknowledge its existence in many of our lives and how much it can color our actions and reactions when our child comes out as transgender. If any of what I described above resonates with you, consider working through this with a trauma-informed therapist. If you are questioning if you should go to therapy, you should probably be going to therapy. Finally, please don't discount the value of community, primarily because many of us who lived through trauma tend to be independent and to hide out of shame. Find a safe, supportive group where you can feel not so alone, because I promise you that you're not alone.

But what about our transgender kids? Are they experiencing trauma and trauma responses from being gender diverse in a world that isn't always kind to transgender people? Absolutely. When our child's brain is in trauma, their amygdala forces their underdeveloped prefrontal cortex offline, and they actually can't learn or think or make decisions. They live in a constant state of fight, flight, or freeze. This can show up as issues at school, problems with concentration, and emotional dysregulation—going from content to enraged in a nanosecond. Side note here: emotional regulation is modeled in caregivers, so if we caregivers lived through trauma, we might not regulate well and therefore can't model emotional regulation.

Here are some signs to keep an eye out for, and note that these can be a repeat of what was already discussed in the 'Signs that something is up' section. When your child is dealing with a trauma response, you can notice either a drop in grades or a hyper-focus on perfectionism. You might see some big ups and downs in emotions to even the smallest of upsets or anxiety, stomach aches, headaches, or illnesses that are not medically explained, school refusal, and issues at school. Your child might also drop activities that they used to enjoy.

Again, how to deal with trauma responses in our children is not something that can be glossed over in a book. If you notice these signs in your child, please consult a gender-diversity-friendly, trauma-aware psychologist.

School issues

Excelling in school and getting into the right college can be a strong family value for many of us. There can also be a cultural or societal drive to have kids as young as toddlers enrolled in the best schools. Some of you might even have purchased your house or rented an apartment specifically to be in a particular school district. After spending so much time and energy securing your child's best possible future through a good education, the last thing you want is to have your child's school experience and grades suffer.

Even if education isn't the top priority for your family, the reality is that school occupies a considerable chunk of our children's lives and therefore is the place where things will show up when something is off for your gender-diverse kid. That can show up as social issues with friends or out-right harassment from bullies, or it can show up as struggles with the learning itself.

We battled both falling grades and social issues at school on Mitchell's journey. We went from Mitchell finishing grade three with a glowing report of how well he got along with his peers and the suggestions that he might benefit from being tested for giftedness to ending grade four with four suspensions for social issues. The social problems continued for several years until he was affirmed entirely as a boy in school in grade seven. His grades were also all over the map. He was put in a special program in grade six for giftedness and then switched schools and struggled to maintain straight Cs, only to make it onto the honor roll in grade ten.

Had I been hyper-focused on Mitchell's grades, I would have been sorely disappointed by the ups and downs and feared for his future post-secondary and job opportunities. But I knew in my heart that I was raising a smart boy. Outside of schoolwork, he was on top of news and social justice topics and could talk circles around most of us when it came to building computers. He was also building his brain in music classes, which I knew would also help him in various ways in the long run. I had to focus on what made him happy, what regulated his emotions, and what physical changes needed to be addressed so that gender dysphoria didn't ruin his life. Once that was all managed, by grade ten, Mitchell focused on school and his future. He started to look at what options he would need to get into university and what programs would lead to the careers he had in mind.

As mentioned in the previous section, signs of trauma can show up as school avoidance and a drop in grades. Even if your child is wholly supported by parents and school-mates, dealing with the stressor of gender dysphoria can also cause kids to be distracted and not performing their best in school. It's important to find the cause of school avoidance and a drop in grades and address that as best as you can. You might also want to explore schooling alterna-tives if regular classroom learning is not working out. Some options include changing to a new school, homeschooling, and online schooling. These don't have to be permanent situations; they can be temporary while your child gets through the most stressful part of transitioning, unless they work better for everyone.

Gender diversity links with neurodiversity

With the remarkable increase in people coming forward as transgender in the past decade, more health professionals are noticing patterns and launching studies. Some of those patterns include gender clinics seeing more gender-diverse kids on the autism spectrum than the general population. Similar observations are being made about more gender-diverse kids being diagnosed with attention deficit hyperac-tivity disorder (ADHD), learning disabilities, or giftedness.

From the studies I have read, and anecdotally from the families I have met with gender-diverse kids, there is an overlap in the occurrence of autism spectrum disorder (ASD) and gender diversity.

The theories as to why the psychological community is finding this link are not definitive yet. A possible explanation is that autistic people do not read social cues in a typical way and therefore do not learn the societal construction of gender the same way a neurotypical person might. Consequently, they are less likely to conform to the gender they were assigned at birth. Or, possibly, the child with neurodiversity has the gift of expansive and creative ways of conceptualizing gender beyond what the general public views as merely male and female. Dr. Diane Ehrensaft noted in a lecture that the occurrence of non-binary identity, agender identity, and gender fluidity among gender-diverse autistic people is greater than the occurrence of binary transition from female to male or male to female. Children with ASD also seem less concerned about gender expression and fitting in to the socially acceptable presentations of gender and are more closely connected to the identity and internal knowing of their gender.

Why would it matter that we know about these links and overlaps? So that we, as parents, can remove the roadblocks to affirming our child's gender identity. I thought that I had to deal with Mitchell's anxiety and depression before addressing his gender diversity, but I needed to address both simultaneously. The same would be true for an autistic child. You can't push aside their need for gender expansion because they are dealing with ASD. They are both very much linked to the core of your child. I know all too well the desire to only have to deal with one issue at a time, but we have to see that the issues are intertwined. It can be tempting for a parent to dismiss a transgender child's constant focus on gender as just another autism obsession phase, but you will recall that gender identity is much more consistent, persistent, and insistent.

Another way this connection matters is that if your child is neurodiverse in any way, they might be less likely to be able to access gender-affirming care on their own. Sadly, all the statistics of increased self-harm and suicide attempts apply here too. As parents and advocates, we want to protect these fantastic humans by removing barriers to care any time we possibly can. The good news is that we have the tools to remove gender dysphoria by affirming a child's gender identity, which may make life with ASD feel smoother.

I shared earlier that a few of Mitchell's teachers used the word gifted when describing him and that he was in a gifted program in grade six. However, we never had him officially tested, and to be honest, I don't feel the need to do so. I didn't want to put academic labels on him that would make him more "different" from his peers than he already was. With everything that Mitchell was facing being a transgender child, I felt that he didn't need the added academic challenges that came with a gifted label. Was I wrong for not pursuing a gifted program for him? Possibly.

But I think we, as parents, need to give ourselves some grace for doing the best we can within the life situations we find ourselves. I am grateful today that I didn't let myself be swayed away from affirming his gender diversity by focusing only on his academic life.

You Time

Admittedly, this chapter covered some serious topics with regards to your child's wellbeing, and now it's time to focus on your own wellbeing. Here are some coaching questions for you to unpack in your journal. Be sure to give yourself a little pocket of quiet and peaceful time today.

1. What was I taught about emotions growing up?

2. How can I get more comfortable with my own emotions and the emotions of others around me?

3. What is it about my child's gender identity that brings up emotions within me?

Chapter 8

◦◦◦◦∞◦◦◦◦

For Now, Not Forever

Even though having your child come out as transgender can feel like your whole life is changing forever, there are temporary parts of this journey. The part where we are unsure, afraid, and do not know what's next is relatively brief. We can fixate on things that don't need as much energy and emotional labor, and in the end, they're not permanent states.

When Mitchell first came out, his main priority was to grow a beard—at eleven. Despite us telling him that no other eleven-year-olds we knew sported a hipster beard, let alone five o'clock shadow, he was very impatient for that stage of transition. A beard was a significant secondary sex characteristic that he identified as being male, and it was crucial to him. This is where we started using the almost daily refrain, "for now, not forever." It was a way to signal to

Mitchell that though he couldn't see a man when he looked at himself in the mirror, that time would come.

Mitchell also couldn't see who he would be as an adult. Initially, he didn't know what career he wanted or if he wanted to get married and have kids one day; it's like his future was completely blacked out for him. That wasn't permanent and mainly occurred in the first year after he came out, but it was scary as a mom to have my child feel so hopeless about the future that he couldn't even imagine one.

As I mentioned earlier, Mitchell's dysphoria settled quite a bit when he was put on hormone blockers. He felt affirmed, he didn't have to deal with a menstrual cycle, and he fitted in with the other boys in his class. Eventually, his classmates had their voices drop, their legs got hairy, and peach-fuzz mustaches started to grow. His dysphoria returned, as did those feelings of hopelessness and not being able to go on. We knew it was time for him to start cross hormones. While we waited for those appointments and decisions to be made by the healthcare team, we repeated over and over again, "This feeling that you have is for now, not forever. One day soon, you will be old enough to qualify for cross hormones. One day, you will be old enough to be eligible for top surgery. Today is just not that day, but that day is coming."

The flip side of the feeling that things will always be the same is the feeling of euphoria when our child is affirmed. Some of us like to call it the champagne-cork effect. Things have been bottled up inside for so long that when our kids disclose, they explode with excitement. When those kids initially come out and are affirmed, they are loud and proud, and they love to let their freak flag fly. This can sometimes be overwhelming to parents because we think our kids will be this intense forever. But even the best champagne loses its fizz eventually. Mitchell physically vibrated. He was so full of frenetic energy when he popped the cork on his metaphorical champagne bottle. It was beautiful to see him so emphatic about how he felt and so happy to be seen and heard for who he was. After a while, I was ready for his energy to settle down. I was concerned that we would spend our whole life talking about being transgender and that it would be woven into every facet of our lives.

And things did eventually settle down. It was like the pendulum swung from not being affirmed, to being loud and proud, to being content and proud. Mitchell is a regular teen boy who cares about social justice and the trans community and likes to play the guitar, video games, and go on family hikes. He doesn't hide that he is a transgender young man, but it's not the only topic of conversation anymore.

When our kids are angry at us

Another phenomenon that is thankfully not forever is that some trans teens and young adults harbor considerable anger for their parents or caregivers. We get the brunt of that anger for a couple of reasons. Sometimes, as parents, we are safe people to be mad at because they know we will always be there. But conversely, sometimes parents represent the oppressive system under which the transgender community must survive. It becomes the phenomenon of punching up that you see in oppressed communities. You might see and hear this if your child participates in groups of transgender activists and progressive advocates. In those groups, they might hear the narrative that all parents are transphobic.

Yes, there are transphobic parents. I am not ashamed to admit that I was transphobic in my initial response to my son's disclosure. I admit to my fear of him being judged and belittled and harassed and having fewer job opportunities and fewer relationship opportunities. These were all founded in "othering" the transgender community. So it's not wrong when the transgender community pegs some parents of trans kids as transphobic, because there are transphobic parents. Some parents start with fears and biases but learn, grow, and become allies. Some parents are rock stars in their allyship and affirmation. And some parents kick their kids out and disown them. But just as gender-diverse people don't want to be painted with the same brush, so too can parents ask to be evaluated on their own merit.

Combine those evil-parent stories with the natural adolescent-developmental stage of exerting independence from their caregivers, and you might face some anger and backlash from your kid. I have heard from and spoken to many parents of trans kids who have experienced this angry rebellion. It can be devastating and hurtful to know that you are doing everything you possibly can to make your child's life better and have your kids not recognize your effort. You use a new name and pronouns, drive them to all the appointments, spend piles of money on clothing accessories and gender-affirming gear, make arrangements with psychologists and gender clinics, and your kid still gets angry with you. Raising a teen isn't easy.

Then there's peer pressure. I remember clearly a conversation that I overheard Mitchell have with his friends from a gender-diversity support group. I could tell that the conversation was about how their parents reacted when they came out. When it was Mitchell's turn to say how I reacted when he came out, I was hurt to hear what he had to say. He viewed my reaction as a bit more dismissive than I thought that I had been. After his phone call, I took him aside for a heart-to-heart. I wanted to know if he genuinely felt that hurt when he came out to me. We had an excellent deep conversation that did eventually circle round to him admitting that he was exaggerating to his friends a little and that I hurt him more than I had initially thought. I share this with you to show the peer pressure aspect of wanting to fit in by punching up at your parents and the reality that we might not even realize the times we are hurting our children inadvertently. Again, that was for then, not forever.

Remembering the other relationships

Having their child disclose their gender diversity can disrupt a parent's everyday life, no matter how affirming they are. If you look at each of the topics in the previous chapters, you can see that there are conversations to have and decisions to make, clothes to buy, schools to inform, and on and on. That's in the best-case scenario when all is well with your child. Add to that any stress from having your child be distressed about their body, socially anxious, depressed, or suicidal, and you've got what can feel like a full-time job and a twenty-four-hour-a-day mental load.

I started to have tunnel vision as I fell into survival mode at the most harried part of our journey. Just like when Mitchell was euphoric and everything was about being transgender, when he was dysphoric, my whole attention was on keeping him safe and doing anything to get my happy-go-lucky child back. It was almost an obsession and a survival instinct blended into one. Much of my response can be explained by the aspects of trauma we covered in the last chapter, but the reality was that my hyper-focus affected the other relationships in my life.

The year Mitchell came out as transgender was a banner year of upheaval in our lives. My husband was diagnosed with colon cancer right as we started Mitchell's social transition and had major abdominal surgery a month before Mitchell's suicide attempt. My oldest child, who lived across the country, battled severe mental health issues. My second oldest child was adjusting to university and changed her program partway through her degree. My mother suddenly passed away, my father's dementia and Parkinson's disease deteriorated, and my youngest child was finally diagnosed with celiac disease. All in one year. And all the while, we were dealing with Mitchell being bullied at one school and switching to a new school and starting hormone blockers, driving across the city to therapy appointments, and learning to affirm him. I should also mention that my personal twisted trauma response was to bury myself in work, so I tripled my business sales that year too. I was absolutely exhausted.

Not surprisingly, by the end of that year, I was tremendously sick. While I recovered, I slowly remembered that survival mode was no way to be in a relationship with my children, spouse, and friends. You will want to be careful not to neglect the other relationships in your life by making everything about your transgender child. And that includes your relationship with yourself. We have heard all the analogies, such as you can't serve from an empty cup, and put your oxygen mask on before assisting others. But they can all sound flat when you are fighting to save your child's life or their social wellbeing.

It was a struggle to divert my attention from Mitchell back to my other kids, but they deserved a mom who was on their side as much as my trans son. I won't even attempt to convince myself I did anything remotely close to a good job of dividing my time and attention equally. It felt a lot like I was juggling. It also felt like any time I focused on things like my husband's battle with colon cancer, Mitchell's dysphoria would worsen. Although I hate living at the other end of the country from my two older kids, it was a bit of a blessing not to have to fit their young-adult goings-on into my overfilled brain on a daily basis.

My husband and I did eventually schedule a few couples counselling sessions to work on our marriage. We worked out some of the differences we faced in terms of the speed with which we each came to a place of surrender and acceptance. We also worked through the distribution of the mental load as I initially made and attended all the appointments until I learned to ask for help. Rod was always willing to help; he was just never given the opportunity.

Co-parenting

While I have experience co-parenting my two oldest children with my ex-husband, this wasn't the case with Mitchell. That being said, through the various peer groups I have attended and led, I have met many parents who have to juggle and negotiate their child's transition with someone they don't want to be married to anymore. I have also seen relationships dissolve after a child comes out because one parent is accepting and the other isn't. Adding new partners and step-parents to the mix only adds more opinions.

I love the word co-parenting because it speaks to a partnership and allyship for the sake of the child or children you have in common. It's teamwork in support of our children. And I have no delusions that there is usually a reason we are parenting apart, which makes co-parenting a unique challenge. While this book is not the essential guide to relationships, we need to realize that raising a gender-diverse child can impact your intimate relationships, and issues with a life partner will affect your ability to support and affirm your child. Imagine the stress on a marriage if one parent is affirming a child when the other isn't. What about the turmoil for a child when they can be out at one parent's home but not the other parent's home? This is very much a reality for many families and an added layer of tension for everyone involved.

Not all relationships are forever. Not only do marriages or partnerships dissolve, but we must also face the reality that our children can also choose not to include us in their lives if it is painful for them to be around us. They may not have the option to walk out as young children, but teens leave home to couch-surf, and young adults can undoubtedly cut ties. As a mother, I will always see myself as my children's mother, but I wouldn't blame my children for avoiding a relationship with me if I was unsupportive or hurtful. It's not guaranteed to be forever both ways. But here's the thing that I learned by co-parenting my first two children: I was not responsible for saving or severing my kids' relationship with their dad. The best advice I was ever given was not to speak ill of my ex-husband around my kids because they would take on those harsh words and because they would eventually see for themselves whatever faults their dad had. (They ultimately saw my flaws too.)

If you are dealing with a problematic co-parenting situation around your child's gender diversity, please put your child's wellbeing ahead of any arguments and "right-fighting," as tempting as they can be. Consider family therapy; it is possible to engage in this even if you are separated. Other options are to use the services of a mediator or, in the worst possible situation, employing a lawyer to protect your child's human rights.

Siblings and extended family relationships

There is a unique quality to a sibling relationship that you don't quite find in any other human bond. Often, these children spend more time together—during their formative years but also over a lifetime—than with other friends or family members. And, of course, sibling relationships can vary widely throughout families. Some are close and skirt the edges of best friends, while others mix as well as oil and water. Because siblings share a significant part of their lives together, you would expect some effect or reaction if one sibling discloses their gender diversity.

Many factors influence a child, teen, or young adult's reaction to learning they have a transgender sibling. Their age, and subsequently their understanding of gender, is one factor. Interestingly, when kids are very young, they are much more open to and fluid with the concept of gender and with change. Today, most kids and teens are more familiar with gender diversity than many adults I know. They quickly understand the terminology and have no issues using pronouns such as they and them. Older siblings who have spent a lifetime addressing their brother as a boy, or even later a man, understandably need a bit more time and patience to process all the changes if she discloses that she is a trans woman. Other factors include how close the relationship was from the beginning and a sibling's traditional belief systems.

For our family, my youngest was nine years old when Mitchell came out as transgender. His response was, "Cool. I always wanted a brother." That was it. From that moment on, he never made a mistake with names or pronouns. Their relationship had always been incredibly close and remained that way. For my second oldest daughter, who had spent most of Mitchell's life doting on him like a second mother, his disclosure wasn't a shock or a surprise but more of a confirmation. She said that she knew there was something there but could never quite put her finger on it. But when I told her Mitchell was a trans boy, she thought, "Of course he is!" She says that it both made sense and felt right. For my oldest child, who happens to be nine years older than Mitchell, there were similar feelings to mine regarding losing the person we had known since birth. Interestingly, a few years after Mitchell started his transition, my oldest child started their own gender exploration and identifies today as non-binary.

As parents, we need to facilitate a way for siblings to express their worries and emotions in a safe space away from our gender-diverse child's eyes and ears. We want to be sure they feel heard and understood. Just as we have some fears of being judged as adults, so too can siblings. We want to provide them with the best information and emotional support so that they can be allies to their sibling. We also need to understand that at some point, we can't control if a sibling relationship blossoms or cools. This can be very difficult for them and for us and might be something to explore in therapy if everyone is willing to try.

While cousins, grandparents, aunts, and uncles may not have as close relationships with your child as siblings who live in the same home, in some families there can be quite close family bonds. I have already covered how to tell your extended family, when your child is ready, in chapter three, but here I want to talk about navigating these relationships, which might become stronger or you might have to create some boundaries around them.

When Mitchell transitioned, my father's memory was unreliable and he often mistook my oldest child for me when either of us visited him. I didn't want to add to any confusion by telling him about the changes in Mitchell's appearance. So, we didn't say anything, and my dad didn't ask. When he saw Mitchell presenting as a boy, he addressed him as if we had always had a boy. My dad passed away a few years later, and I always regretted not having that conversation with him so that he would have known Mitchell authentically for who he is.

My mom lived across the country but had visited us just one month before Mitchell came out as transgender. When I told her over the phone about him, her response was, "I don't care what she says. She will always be my granddaughter." My momma bear hackles went up, and I let my mom know in no uncertain terms that he was to be addressed as a boy. Period. What I didn't fully appreciate at the time was my mother's grieving process, as I was fully enveloped in my own while still trying to protect my child. The emotions and questions that we, as parents and caregivers, process— messily and in a nonlinear fashion—are the same emotions that siblings and extended family experience. Everything that I covered in chapter one can easily be felt to varying degrees by other close members of the family. We all deserve a little bit of grace in the beginning, as long as it's away from the transgender person's eyes and ears.

My mom passed away suddenly from anaphylactic shock only six months after that phone conversation and never got to see and know Mitchell as his authentic self. My husband's parents had already died before Mitchell was born, and that left only my sister and and my husband's remaining five brothers to inform and walk through using the correct name and pronoun.

Our boundaries were clear that everyone was to accept, affirm, and address Mitchell as a boy. Those clear expectations on everyone, with gentle reminders if there were pronoun and name slip-ups, helped Mitchell feel safe within our family. I have noticed a closeness develop within the family between certain members who are more willing to be vulnerable and authentic. We were fortunate that most older relatives were accepting, but we know of others who have had to cut ties with unmovable mindsets.

Forever

While some stages of transition are temporary and merely require a little patience on everyone's part, others are permanent. The sooner you see your child as any other child and normalize your life, the easier things get. I made a mistake early on, and have seen some parents do the same, which was to walk on eggshells around my kid, afraid to say or do anything that might offend, hurt, or trigger a mood. Our kids are not broken. Yes, they might be processing a colossal life change, but that doesn't mean they can't unload the dishwasher or vacuum their rooms.

I clearly remember having a conversation during a mental health visit to urgent care with Mitchell in one of his episodes of profound hopelessness. We just happened to have a gay man as a doctor who reminded Mitchell of his protective factors, meaning what was worth living for, and that life does get better. By this time, I was plainly tired of reminding Mitchell that one day he would be seen as a man by everyone and that the drama of middle school would be long behind him. I appreciated the reinforcements of a doctor who shared that his love of Madonna in middle school made him odd in the eyes of his classmates, but today it's one of the quirks his friends and partner love most.

While we all saw some lightness return to Mitchell's shoulders by the end of the consultation, I wasn't quite as relieved as him. The doctor asked me about my own experience and burden. I shared how exhausted I was trying to raise a preteen in general, besides all the gender-diversity add-ons. I shared that I was afraid to ask Mitchell to clean his room or do his laundry and have that be the thing that set him off into suicidal ideation or self-injury, and I got the best and most straightforward advice, "Just ask him to clean his room. He still has to learn to be a decent human being on this planet. That includes being decent in your home and cleaning his room before the rotting food attracts bugs. You are addressing his moods and affirming his transition. None of that has to stop him from washing his socks."

Nothing he said was revolutionary to me. I have raised four children, and I fully understand how to set expectations and the benefits of instilling my values in my children. But I did need that reminder. I am raising a regular human being who needs to operate within society.

I temporarily forgot the emotional safety and trust that our children sense when we have consistent expectations. There is a comfort to the setting of boundaries. Our children have enough to be anxious about as they explore their gender in a society in which expectations of gender roles may not match. The least we can do to help ease some anxiety is to keep our rules and expectations consistent.

Here are some guidelines if your child is dealing with strong emotions that make you question how you can create discipline in your home. You already know this. Read it as a reminder. Clearly communicate the expectations. When possible, offer some choices of what the chore will be or when it will happen. You can also have them come up with an alternative and talk about the consequences of those choices. Establish how they want to be reminded of their chore and the effects of not doing them. Remember, by following through consistently on the consequences, we are offering stability and teaching them how the world operates. Out in the community, we all stop on red and go on green no matter how much our feelings are hurt that day.

It is absolutely okay to comfort your child who is living through a difficult emotional time. I highly encourage that we help our children process difficult emotions. But that doesn't mean that your boundaries and rules have to change. This is a "yes-and" situation, not an "either-or" one. "Yes, I see that you are very sad about what Jamie said yesterday, and today you are going to mow the lawn."

Of course, you will want to wait until emotions are not volatile to have discussions around expectations, chores, or boundaries. Have the conversation when the moment is not heated, so your child is not in a situation of high or low emotion and you not angry, frustrated, or exhausted.

One last consideration is that this is not a phase. While

in the beginning, when I didn't understand and let fear rule my life, I hoped that Mitchell would grow out of "the idea that he was transgender," Mitchell will be a trans man for the rest of his life. What I want for my son is what all parents and caregivers wish for their kids—health, happiness, love, acceptance, and to thrive in whatever life or career he wants to create for himself. To support him in that, as a parent, I need to prepare him for adulthood. For our gender-diverse kids, it might mean a few extra considerations or life lessons, but that doesn't mean that we skip over how to balance a cheque book or when to change the oil in our car. The sooner you can embrace that this is forever, the easier it will be on everyone.

You Time

Relationships are the spice of life, aren't they? As humans, we are social beings and long to belong, yet nothing challenges us more than being in a relationship with others. Take a few minutes with your cup of tea and favorite pen and go deep answering these coaching questions.

1. Reflect back on each relationship in this chapter and assess how the relationships worked before your

child's gender-diversity disclosure. What has changed? What has stayed the same?

2. Where do I need to feel heard?

3. What do I need to say that can't be said?

4. Where do I need to listen more?

Chapter 9

❧

Beyond the First Hundred Days

When I first thought of writing this book, I considered calling it "What to do in the first hundred days after your child comes out as transgender." A friend of mine suggested that title. She is a psychologist and had recently attended a conference where someone spoke on what to do in the first hundred days after your child is diagnosed with autism. I thought it was a brilliant idea because those first three months can be overwhelming—between dealing with your own emotions and ensuring that you are taking care of your child's emotional, psychological, and physical wellbeing. You drink from a fire hose of information, from learning how to change your kid's name at school to how to buy a new gender-affirming bathing suit.

But the reality is that we, as parents, still need support

beyond those first three months. I surely wasn't ready to unpack all of the information in this book over that short amount of time. In the end, there is no timeline for your transgender child, just like there is no set timeline for you. As I've mentioned before, some kids are happy to only change up their gender expression and some kids transition much faster. Some of us parents come into this from a place of immediate acceptance and march down to the nearest gender clinic immediately, while some of us navigate changes at a different pace.

This chapter looks at what's it's like to parent a transgender child a little later in their journey—after the social transition and past the resistance that this could be a phase.

A peek at hormones and surgery

The day we left the gender clinic with an appointment to start cross hormones, Mitchell's feet barely touched the ground in the parking garage on our way back to the car. I felt like I was trudging through molasses. Yet, I had a smile on my face. I said all the right encouraging words, but I carried the weight of responsibility deep down inside. I was about to consent to permanently altering my child's body.

A friend of mine once told me that when she discussed our family with her brother, he said that I should be in jail for child abuse for allowing my son to transition. I had read similar comments on social media, but it bore an extra sting from the mouth of someone I knew. Until the nurse made the appointment to start testosterone, Mitchell's whole transition was reversible. Once you stop hormone blockers, puberty resumes. I could paint his room pink again. We could buy a new dress. That was my out card. I wasn't responsible for a permanent change, only responsible for making my child happy.

The plan to start testosterone filled me with fear because I felt like I would soon be responsible for altering my child. As if my husband, the doctor, the psychiatrist, the therapist, and, most importantly, my son didn't have a part to play in this decision.

To alleviate the unbearable weight of responsibility on my chest, I sat alone on my couch and played the what-if game. I asked myself, "What if he was born with a congenital disability? Would I agree to lifelong medication and surgery?" You bet I would! In a heartbeat. So how was this any different? He was born with the wrong endocrine glands secreting the wrong hormone for his brain. The doctors are giving him the right hormone. Just like a person with diabetes is given insulin. It's not that radical when I think of it that way.

In the beginning, my problem was that I thought being transgender had an element of choice. Not necessarily that my son was choosing to be a boy instead of a girl, but that we had a choice in terms of how fast or slow he transitioned and a choice to "just dress like a boy" vs. medical intervention. It took me living with him through his body dysphoria to realize that this was not a choice I got to make for my son. We must ask ourselves: at what point does a child have ownership of their own body or life?

The whole experience of parenting is the struggle to choose when to let our children be independent. At what age do we let them cross the street without holding our hand? When do we let them take the bus on their own? When do we let them drive alone? Add to that self-governing in medical decisions. At what age are you comfortable with your child seeing their doctor without you in the room? It may feel like never, but there are rules about when they can legally ask you to leave.

When it came to my son having autonomy in the medical decision to start testosterone, I had to remind myself that he was making those decisions with a medical doctor—a doctor who is using guidelines provided by scientific studies and supported by the World Health Organization, World Professional Association for Transgender Health and University of California San Francisco (UCSF) protocols. My friend's brother may call it child abuse, but that is an opinion based on his beliefs and feelings. It is not based on science.

Much like the legality of name and gender-marker changes, the medical options for affirming your child's gender depend on where you live. In some countries or states, it is illegal to use hormone blockers or cross hormones or perform any gender-affirming surgeries on people under the age of 18. These interventions are legal in other countries or states, but they're not covered by private or public health insurance. In Canada, medical appointments and surgeries are covered by universal healthcare but at the time of writing this book, medication is not. Some people are lucky enough to have health insurance through their employer that covers some of the medication costs.

Here are the costs of some transgender-affirming medications in my home province in 2021.

- Lupron (hormone blocker injection): $5000/year
- Testosterone injections: $50–90 for a three-month supply
- Testosterone gel or patch: $125/month
- Spironolactone (male hormone suppressant): $20/month
- Estrace (pill): $20–40/month
- Estrogen patch: $25–50/month
- Estrogen gel: $40–80/month

I know there can be some sticker shock at those expenses, especially if you don't have any healthcare coverage. But as I wrote earlier, if my child were diabetic or had any other condition that required regular medication, I wouldn't hesitate to pay for his drugs and find a way to get coverage. Once a medical team has determined that hormone blockers and cross hormones are warranted, we need to understand their essential value to our child's wellbeing. This is not a frivolous choice; your kid is not asking you for the latest pair of sneakers or video games. As part of the routine of being on hormone blockers and cross hormones, your child will be seen by an endocrinologist and have blood tests regularly.

I had been warned by a transgender man long before we even considered medication that there were often manufacturer shortages of testosterone. Just this past month, I heard from a parenting group that there was a manufacturer shortage of Lupron. Shortages can be scary. It means that your child can finally be happy and comfortable in their body but have that threatened by a lack of availability of the very thing that makes them comfortable. Doctors prescribe different types of hormones or hormone blockers or switch from a three-month-long dose to a monthly amount when these shortages happen. I can tell you I don't like having the stress of changing things around all the time. Be aware that this is an inconvenience that can arise.

Looking down the road at surgery means waiting until your child is an adult in most districts. There are places where your child could qualify for top surgery, either chest masculinization or breast augmentation, before 18, but that is not currently universal, even in Canada. Who can refer your child for surgery and how long they need to have been on hormones if at all changes from one location to another, so your best bet is to gather all of this information from a gender clinic in your home province, state, or country.

One final thought on hormones and surgery is that in Canada, at least, there are waitlists that are sometimes up to two years long, depending on provincial funding for gender clinics. If you know that this is an option you'd like to explore with your child in the future, it might be worth getting on one of those waitlists in the meantime. You can always ask to be removed if anything changes or your child's turn comes up too quickly.

It gets better

There is so much that I know now and I wish I'd known five years ago. While it hasn't always been a walk in the park, and some of my worst fears did make brief appearances, there is so much more happiness to our story than I ever could have imagined the day my child told me he was transgender. But there is a natural human tendency to have a negative bias. When we think of the future, we list off all the things that can go wrong instead of all the things that can go right. I worried that my son would never find a job, that he wouldn't be loved and find a life partner, or that if he did find the love of his life, the in-laws wouldn't accept him. I worried about outright bullying and harassment, that he would lose all his friends, and that I would lose all of mine. I didn't realize there were new friends that I would make because Mitchell was transgender.

There are important people in my life today that I would never have gotten to know if not for Mitchell. He can say the same thing. He's had many opportunities, from speaking at a Pride festival to being on discussion panels. He's worked as a music teacher and is a sought-after babysitter in the neighborhood. He's had reciprocated romantic attractions, though I am not rushing any relationship goals at sixteen. And Mitchell is not an anomaly.

We've even gotten to a lot better at balancing appointments and needles. I recently brought Mitchell to the gender clinic at the children's hospital, where we've been regular patrons for close to five years. I thought back to the first bunch of appointments and how stressed and anxious I was about being on time and where to show up. It's all routine now. Even needles are a non-issue today, compared with all the accommodations we had in place so that Mitchell wouldn't pass out or throw up during his shot or blood tests. I am not joking. We had to put topical cream to freeze the area, then ice, then a buzzy contraption that vibrated, then a lollipop, and finally a countdown. Now it's just looking away and poke, we're done.

The more I volunteer and work in the LGBTQIA+ community, the more I learn about the positive stories that rarely make the news. If you look for them, you will find the stories of children who are welcomed into their classes and teams, children who become artists, entrepreneurs, professionals, and even parents themselves.

How I feel today is a far cry from the emotions I cycled

through during the first chapter in the first part of this journey. I no longer deal with doubt or feel overwhelmed from it all; I occasionally get a twinge of sadness, but it is rare and short-lived. I avoided Facebook memories for years because I didn't want to see old pictures of my child before his transition, but today I have no issue with old photos. We still don't post pictures of him before transition anywhere, but I have them stowed away for safekeeping if Mitchell ever wants them one day. The emotion that has changed the most for me is the frustration with feeling like I was constantly coming out to people and the vulnerability that came with it from not knowing how people would react and not truly understanding what I was telling people.

Today, I am grateful for this whole experience. I am much more courageous when talking about gender diversity and sharing our family's experiences. I understand why some people have narrow-minded views, and I don't find them threatening. Maybe because I know my son so well, and I don't doubt that what we are doing is right for his health and happiness for a second. Through all the people I have met since becoming an advocate, I know that gender-diverse kids are phenomenal youth who grow into amazing adults. We are all enriched by knowing them.

Advocacy work

Some advocacy work we jump into as parents and caregivers on day one of our child coming out as transgender, which includes being a supporter of their wellbeing and correcting people who use stigmatizing terms. You may want to put other aspects of advocacy work on hold until the more emergent and harried parts of the social transition are behind you. Once ready, you can volunteer for a local LGBTQIA+ organization, fundraise for awareness or for capital for transgender gear for kids who can't afford it, and write to your local, state, or provincial politicians to ask for changes in legislation or human rights protection. This is also where you could start a letter-writing campaign to those medication manufacturers too.

Before you start, know your motivation. It can vary from wanting to participate in the trans community to wanting to improve conditions for your child. This can be tiring work, and most of it is done voluntarily by other similarly overextended volunteers. By knowing and connecting to your motivation, you can find the energy to keep soldiering on when times get tough. You'll also want sincerity of beliefs. I could not have been a strong advocate in the beginning when I wasn't sure what it meant to be transgender. Only when I was further along in Mitchell's transition and fully understood gender identity was I firm in my beliefs of dignity and equity. Finally, advocate when you are ready to stand up for more than just your child. Of course, we all start out advocating for our kids. Momma bear wants to keep her cubs safe. But, the greatest benefit of your time in the world of advocacy is ensuring that policies get changed for the whole community.

This isn't for everyone, and that's okay. You don't have to run for office or start a non-profit organization. It's enough to stay educated on gender-diversity topics and stand up when you can to give voice to those who are not being heard.

Finally, Mitchell mentioned a phrase I like to use often in his foreword—"Not about us without us." Advocacy work is very much needed, but we can't do it at the expense of drowning out the voices of the very people we are trying to lift. If there is a transgender person who is ready, willing, and able to advocate for the community, please include them in your work. As a woman, I don't want to hear from a man what childbirth or menopause feels like. A person of color doesn't want to hear about the experience of racism from a white person. The same applies to gender-diverse individuals. Advocacy also means handing them the microphone.

Returning to your self

One day this will all be a memory. Of course, you still see and interact with this memory every day, granted, but the upheaval will be over. That's when you eventually sit down with yourself and ask, "What about me?" and, "What's next?"

When we deal with any family change or crisis, it's easy for us parents and caregivers to be focused on keeping our children safe and happy. But eventually, our kids settle into their everyday lives. For some of us, this ends up looking like empty-nest syndrome, and others of us have found our groove by the time our child is a teenager. In my case, this happened when Mitchell was fifteen, but I was coming back to myself as a changed person.

There are so many facets to our lives we could focus on when we choose to retreat inward and regroup that it can be overwhelming. This an exercise I use with coaching clients that you can easily do on your own. Pull out a journal and a pen and let's have a good look at all aspects of your life. I like to use these ten categories, but if I am missing something feel free to add more.

- Health
- Finances
- Fun
- Career
- Romantic relationship(s)
- Family
- Friends
- Hobbies
- Living space
- Spirituality/personal growth

Take a good long look at each of these categories and rate them on a scale of zero to ten, zero being abysmal satisfaction and ten being ultimately satisfied. Note that the scale is on satisfaction here. You get to define for yourself what satisfaction and success mean to you. For example, someone can feel completely satisfied with their finances with $5000 in their savings account, while someone else can feel completely dissatisfied with $500,000. That's entirely up to you and your core values. Let's unpack these categories to help you find the deeper meaning for your unique situation.

Health: This can be a broad category and includes your physical and mental wellbeing. Have you let a chronic illness go unchecked for a long time? Have you escaped the stresses of life through less than healthy food, like I did? Have you overindulged in other numbing behaviors? When we are focused on keeping our children safe, we can easily neglect our own wellbeing. On a scale of zero to ten, how satisfied are you with your health?

Finances: Raising a transgender child can be an expensive adventure. Even though you can find affordable options when it comes to redecorating a bedroom or changing out a wardrobe, you may not have planned for those expenses. Later on, there might be medical and psychological appointments that may or may not be covered by your healthcare insurance. All that being said, money is not always a strong value for some people. On a scale of zero to ten, how satisfied are you with your finances?

Fun: When was the last time you allowed yourself to have unbridled, spontaneous joy and pleasure? When we are dealing with life-altering circumstances, and for some of us, depressed and anxious kids, fun can be quite low on our to-do list. Even without raising a trans child, our society is set up to reward hard work and life plans and not always open to lighthearted abandon. So much so that some of us aren't even sure what constitutes fun. On a scale of zero to ten, how satisfied are you with the amount of fun you are having in your everyday life?

Career: Have you taken a sabbatical, been putting in the bare minimum at work, put off plans for advancement, or put off returning to your career altogether? Maybe you are ready to explore a career change, one that is more in alignment with what you've learned about yourself on this journey with your child. And possibly you've been a stay-at-home parent and are ready to go back to school, or you're ready to retire. On a scale of zero to ten, how satisfied are you with your career or work life?

Romantic relationship(s): Yet another category that can be placed on the backburner while you adjust to a new life with a gender-diverse child. But your relationship with your significant other can be so important to your overall happiness. Maybe you've been single and are ready to start dating again. Maybe you've gotten into a rut of familiarity and need to explore some variety. You might even have opened your mind to exploring a new sexual orientation or determined that you are asexual or aromantic. On a scale of zero to ten, how satisfied are you with your romantic relationship or polyamorous relationships?

Family: I've covered family relationships quite a bit already in this book in terms of how they are affected by your child's transition and healthy boundaries when they are not affirming. Here, you want to have a look at what you can control, which is how much you are reaching out to and interacting with family who are supportive or your other children who need your attention. Have you pushed aside relationships that are worth revisiting now that you are have the emotional reserves to answer questions? Do you need to have more firm boundaries with others? On a scale of zero to ten, how satisfied are you with your family relationships?

Friends: It is a common reaction to push friends aside while we are confronting a stressful situation. While isolating yourself may not be the healthiest response, the reality might be that you did this. Is it time to reach out to friends you haven't seen in a while? Is it time to make new friends whose values and mindsets align with yours? On a scale of zero to ten, how satisfied are you with your friendships?

Hobbies: Along the lines of having fun, hobbies tend to be things that get pushed to the wayside when we are hitting speed bumps in life. I differentiate hobbies from fun because some hobbies are more about relaxation. Is it time for you to connect to your creative side again? Would you like to learn a new skill or craft? On a scale of zero to ten, how satisfied are you with your hobbies?

Living space: Your physical environment might be very important to you. And if you are not an avid Home and Garden Television viewer, you might just need a bit of order in your home. I firmly believe that hiring a housekeeper to clean your home is a mental health tool. Even if it's once a quarter or once a year. Are you a gardener longing to freshen up your yard again? Have you put off repairing that kitchen cabinet door with the loose hinge? Maybe you are finally ready to move to a different neighborhood or country. On a scale of zero to ten, how satisfied are you with your physical environment?

Spirituality or personal growth: Even without having a religious or spiritual practice, everyone can participate in personal growth, whether it is reading self-help books, attending workshops or retreats, or taking an online course. Have you put your self-fulfillment learning on hold to attend to your child's needs? Depending on your religion or spiritual practice, you might be looking for a new way to connect to a higher power without a judgment-laced sermon attached. You deserve to have a place to worship that is inclusive of your child, and they do exist. On a scale of zero to ten, how satisfied are you with your spiritual life and personal growth?

Once you have given each of these aspects of your life a score, have a look at which ones scored the lowest. They are now your priority. Also, you do not have to wait until your child is euphoric and all is wonderful in their world before doing this exercise and working on the parts of your life that need improving. You matter. A happy well-adjusted parent can serve their child much better than an exhausted and frustrated one. While your child is transitioning to their authentic self, you too can transition to a fulfilled and authentic person with them.

Because of this proverbial bus ride that I've been on with my son, my priorities changed, my outlook on life has altered a little, and I have a greater appreciation for disenfranchised people. I am also a whole lot braver than before my son's transition. Having to come out to everyone who knew that I once had a daughter and now have a son was excellent exposure therapy for fear of what people thought. I wear much thicker skin today to the slings and arrows of others' opinions. That also seeped into my professional life. I decided to self-publish a romance novel I had written a decade prior. Before Mitchell came out, I fretted over what people would think of me if I published it, but the truth was that I love writing, and I felt that it was a good book. If a handful of people also enjoyed the escapism for a few hours, why not publish it?

I carry myself with much more confidence with my coaching clients and in networking meetings. I also focused my attention on taking care of my body after years of dealing with my emotions through food. Once I regained my vitality, I stood taller, and a glow returned to my eyes.

That's not to say that I don't still walk alongside my son on his journey. I still attend his medical appointments, take him for blood tests, give him his shots. I still make arrangements for any therapy appointments he needs. But I don't see this as any different from if my son had any other well-managed medical condition. I am still a responsible parent caring for my child while enjoying other relationships, participating in my career, and caring for myself.

A very long time ago, when I first started as a life coach, I wrote an article for *Huffington Post* redefining self-care. It was a concept I've needed to return to over and over throughout the past five years. I know that for many of us, self-care can sound selfish and does not come easily when our kids are struggling. But I urge you to book a babysitter if your child is too young to be home alone and schedule some time to nurture your needs; you will be more helpful to your child.

Here is a list of self-care options that don't have to cost a lot of time or money.

- Go for coffee alone
- Wander through a museum or a bookstore alone
- Take a long bubble bath
- Go to the gym
- Draw, color, or paint
- Learn yoga
- Dance it out
- Get a massage
- Head out into nature
- Start a meditation practice

Finally, find your community. After all of this, your circle of friends might change. Not only because some people quietly, or not so graciously, let themselves out of your life, but also because you will meet new people. It can be way too tempting to isolate ourselves when times are stressful and unsure, but as people we need to be part of a group. So, if you turtled during the most harried parts of this, it's time to get out and see people again. I love how Brené Brown describes the difference between belonging and fitting in. She says that fitting in is assessing a group of people and changing who you are to conform to that group (Brown 2019). Conversely, true belonging never asks us to change who we are; it demands authenticity. In the end, isn't that what our gender-diverse kids teach us the most, to be our authentic selves to belong instead of taking on a role to fit in?

I intended this whole book to focus on your journey as a parent or caregiver in service of both your child's wellbeing and yours. Together we have explored the changes you need to make to affirm your child, teen, or young person's gender diversity. I have also included reminders to check in with yourself so that you can best serve your child. I truly hope you haven't just skipped over those sections, but I can't blame you if you have. I know very well the single-mindedness we face as parents when we are concerned for our children. But, it's not too late. You can access all of the You Time questions in one printable download on my website: www.tammyplunkett.com/beyond-pronouns-workbook.

With these final journal questions, I am asking you to

focus on your whole being and not just the parts of you that are a caregiver to a gender-diverse person. These are the big questions where you must focus entirely on yourself. If it feels uncomfortable and selfish, then so be it. Feel that niggle of selfishness and do it anyway. You deserve this focus because you matter.

You Time

1. What do I want in my life?

2. How do I want to feel every day? Why?

3. What do I love to do?

4. What makes me happy?

5. What does a meaningful life mean to me?

6. How can I live more aligned with my desired meaningful life?

7. What do I want to be remembered for?

8. What problem do I want to solve for others in my work life?

9. How will I know when I'm on the path to success?

10. How will it change my life to be on that path?

11. What do I need to believe to be happy on that path?

12. What is the legacy I want to leave to my family, friends, and the world?

Frequently Asked Questions

What do all the letters in LGBTQQIAAP2S+ mean?

Lesbian, gay, bisexual, transgender, queer, questioning, Intersex, ally, asexual, pansexual, two-spirit, and the plus sign includes any other gender identity or sexual orientation not listed. You may have noticed that I use the abbreviated LGBTQIA+ throughout this book. I chose to do this for simplicity and consistency.

Why are there so many labels, and why do we keep adding more?

Labels are for people in the gender-diverse community to identify with and not for others to impose on them. Claiming and reclaiming a label is empowering to the

LGBTQIA+ community. When someone sees their identity in the acronym, they can see that they are not alone. By adding more letters, we are honoring more identities and sexual orientations.

Is non-binary always considered transgender?

Non-binary fits under the umbrella of transgender in that it fits the definition of someone not identifying with the gender assigned to them at birth. Sometimes, people assume that transgender means going from one gender to the other such as male to female, and it can mean that, but it also encapsulates all gender diversity. Other gender-diversity labels include gender fluid, gender creative, agender and more.

How can a child be transgender?

There is a difference between gender identity and sexual orientation. Unfortunately, gender diversity has been lumped in with sexual orientation, and society has conflated the two. In the past, we mixed being transgender with the old term transvestite and associated cross-dressing with a sexual perversion. So, if someone says that a child is transgender and you automatically associate that with a TV show that you watched in the 1980s that showed a cross-dresser as a gay man who was acting out a sexual fetish, then, of course, it sounds absurd that a child could be transgender. The problem is that some people have not learned the real meaning of gender diversity and are using outdated and outright wrong terms of reference. Being transgender also does not mean that a person has to have surgery or even take hormones. A child can be transgender by merely changing their gender expression—their clothes, mannerisms, name, and pronouns.

Is this a phase?

Because more kiddos and teens are coming out as transgender, many people ask if this is just the "in" thing to do. I can tell you that identity, meaning what we truly know about ourselves, is not just a phase. Gender expression, however, can change. We can feel like presenting in a more feminine way one day, and in a more neutral way another day, and maybe more masculine later. The fact that more people are represented in the LGBTQIA+ community in public also gives more words to feelings that people have had for years. There are more words in our vocabulary now that can be associated with people's gender not conforming to what society expects or their gender not confirming what was assigned at birth. Having representation in the community is empowering people to live their authentic truth. It is not causing more people to try to fit into a mold that they do not match. Quite the opposite, it is allowing people to be who they truly are.

Is there something wrong with my child?

There is a difference between children exploring their gender expression and experiencing gender dysphoria. While there will be a need for a medical diagnosis to access medical care and for some legal definitions, you do not need to rush to a doctor or psychologist if your child is happy and healthy. Being transgender is not a mental illness. However, transgender people, like everyone else, can face mental health challenges and neurodiversity. If your child is suffering from unease about their physical body and its functions or generalized dissatisfaction with life, you may want to find a therapist who is well versed in gender identity or a gender clinic near you.

My kid came out as bisexual, then non-binary, and now trans. What's up with that?

One of the Qs in the LGBTQIA+ acronym is for questioning, and that is a legitimate position to allow for our children. This doesn't mean that your child is confused. It means that your child knows that they do not live on the binary's extreme and they know that they're not cisgender or straight. It could also be possible that your child is coming out slowly by dipping their toe into the pool of what is acceptable and not acceptable in your family. If you are not fazed by them coming out as bisexual, they know that they can be safe to come out as non-binary. Then, if they come out as non-binary and see that you are accommodating the changes they need to affirm them, they might feel safe enough to explore their true gender and authenticity.

How do I know if my beliefs or actions are hurting my child?

You might think that you are putting up a good front and fighting some of your biases against any other community than the one you believe is right. Still, it will seep through in your language. It will show in the jokes you laugh at, in the comments that you allow to slide in your presence, and sometimes in your own commentary. Those microaggressions are painful to your child, and they signal to your child that it is not safe for them to come out to you or confide in you. If you are not affirming for your child, you will know by the painful look in their eyes, how they avoid you and hide things from you, and ultimately in their mental health. If they end up having more anxiety or depression, having suicidal thoughts, or self-harm, it is so imperative that you deal with your own beliefs away from your child and affirm them as soon as you possibly can.

What is a microaggression?

I like to think of microaggressions as death by a thousand papercuts. A microaggression is often unintended harm, such as a vague statement or a subtle comment that could seem quite innocent when taken out of context. It can also be passed off as a joke, but the person on the receiving end is not laughing. For example, telling a trans boy to "grow a pair" or a trans woman to be grateful she doesn't experience menstrual cramps can sound innocuous, but they are harsh reminders of a person's gender diversity. Any statement that shows a bias or "othering" is a microaggression.

Where do we start a child's transition?

The first change you make is a social change—usually using a different pronoun. A huge misconception is associating being transgender with permanent physical changes. Not all transgender individuals take hormones or have surgery as adults, and though it may not always be evident to some, children are not having gender-affirming surgery. Their bodies are still growing and developing. It is important to realize that even when teens qualify for potential medical intervention, depending on where they live, there might still be a waitlist to access care. Initially, there is only a social transition that changes their presentation and expression of their gender in the world, none of which is permanent.

How do I access peer support for my child or myself?

You can search for a local PFLAG group or local Pride association. You can also search for a gender clinic, as they might have a group that they can refer you to. Be careful with ad-hoc online groups and choose one with good moderators checking for discrimination or bullying.

What do I do if my child's friend comes out to me and doesn't feel safe to tell their parents?

Studies show that having at least one person in the child's life who is safe and affirming can reduce suicidality to the same rate as the general teen population (The Trevor Project 2021; Olson *et al.* 2016). If you can affirm your child's friend, you are a superhero in my view. You can also get the child to a place where they feel comfortable sharing their truth with their parent. If it is clear that the parents or caregivers will be intolerable and hurtful, you can help the child find the support of a social worker. Sometimes, the best thing we can do to help friends is to find them the best help.

Where can I find trans-specific sexual health education for my child?

There are many websites and organizations that specialize in sexual health education and consider the age of the child and diversity in gender or sexual orientation. One of my favorites is www.amaze.org because of its friendliness to the younger crowds, and it can be viewed in smaller bites.

Gender-diverse sexual health needs to walk the fine line between affirming a person's identity and keeping in mind the biology involved and the different precautions needed for each body type. Finally, all sex education should include information on consent.

How can I be a good ally in the community?

To be a good ally in the community, you can use your pronouns when you introduce yourself, in your email signature, or on a name tag. You can ask people for their pronouns when you introduce yourself. It's a sign of respect that shows you don't assume that their pronouns are automatically she and her because someone is presenting femininely. You can call out bias and discriminatory speech as soon as you hear it and shut down jokes about the transgender community. You can tell happy stories and good stories about the community, and not only the horror stories. There are many happy tales that show that gender-diverse people are whole instead of "othering" the trans community. You can raise money for charities that finance surgeries, medications and transgender gear. You can write letters to your governmental body to ensure that human rights are protected. You can volunteer locally at a Pride association. You can be a true friend and offer a sense of belonging.

References

Bauer, G.R., Scheim, A.I., Pyne, J., Travers, R. and Hammond, R. (2015) 'Intervenable factors associated with suicide risk in transgender persons: A respondent driven sampling study in Ontario, Canada.' *BMC Public Health* *15*, 1.

Brown, B. (2019) 'True belonging is the spiritual practice of...'. Accessed on 12/10/2021 at www.youtube.com/watch?v=dWZa3wm1Nns.

Garriguet, D. (2021) 'Chapter 1: Health of Youth in Canada' In: *Portrait of Youth in Canada: Data Report.* Accessed on 12/10/2021 at www150.statcan.gc.ca/n1/pub/42-28-0001/2021001/article/00001-eng.htm.

Obama, M. (2018) *Becoming.* Toronto: Random House.

Olson, K.R., Durwood, L., DeMeules, M. and McLaughlin, K.A. (2016) 'Mental health of transgender children who are supported in their identities.' *Pediatrics* *137*, 3.

Taylor, A.B., Chan, A., Hall, S.L., Saewyc, E.M. and Canadian Trans & Non-binary Youth Health Survey Research Group (2020) *Being Safe, Being Me 2019: Results of the Canadian Trans and Non-binary Youth Health Survey.* Vancouver: Stigma and Resilience Among Vulnerable Youth Centre, University of British Columbia.

The Trevor Project (2021) *2021 National Survey on LGBTQ Youth Mental Health.* West Hollywood: The Trevor Project.

Resources

Where to find support

There are organizations specifically geared towards supporting parents and caregivers, such as **PFLAG** in the United States: www.pflag.org and in Canada: www.pflagcanada.ca, and **FFLAG** in the UK: www.fflag.org.uk.

Also, many local Pride organizations have parent support groups. You can look up your city's Pride group and ask if they have support for parents.

For transgender-specific crisis intervention, which offers direct emotional and financial support to trans people in crisis, for the trans community, by the trans community, you can find your country's crisis line phone number from **Trans Lifeline**: www.translifeline.org, or **Switchboard LGBT+ Helpline**: https://switchboard.lgbt and **Mindline Trans+**: www.mindinsomerset.org.uk in the UK.

The Trevor Project is the leading organization in the United States providing crisis intervention and suicide-prevention services to lesbian, gay, bisexual, transgender, queer, and questioning young people under 25. Find more information here: www.thetrevorproject.org.

Where to find general information

As a dynamic media force, **GLAAD** tackles tough issues to shape the narrative and provoke dialogue that leads to cultural change. You can find resources here: www.glaad.org.

Gender Creative Kids is a reference community organization that has supported trans, non-binary, and gender-fluid youth's affirmation within their families, schools, and communities: www.gendercreativekids.com.

Gender Spectrum works to create gender-sensitive and inclusive environments for all children and teens. It has a website section devoted to parents and caregivers here: www.genderspectrum.org/audiences/parents-and-family.

If you are looking for how to make changes to identification and legal names changes in Canada, **Skipping Stone** has a fulsome document here: www.skippingstone.ca/idamendments.

In the United States, you can find more information about the legal requirements for identification changes here: www.transequality.org/documents.

Information about legal name changes in the United

Kingdom can be found here: www.deedpoll.org.uk/advice-for-transgender-adults-children.

Where to find healthcare information

The World Professional Association for Transgender Health (**WPATH**) is a non-profit, interdisciplinary professional and educational organization devoted to transgender health and publishes the Standards of Care and Ethical Guidelines on its website: www.wpath.org.

University of California San Francisco (**UCSF**) offer guidelines for the primary and gender-affirming care of transgender and gender non-binary people. The UCSF Gender Affirming Health Program is a multidisciplinary program consisting of experts in transgender medicine and surgery at UCSF Medical Center. For more information on its guidelines visit: https://transcare.ucsf.edu/guidelines.

Trans Youth CAN! is a study of youth referred for blockers or hormones at ten clinics in Canada. It is studying the health experiences of trans youth during the first two years on puberty blockers or hormones and its updated findings are posted regularly at: www.transyouthcan.ca.

Miscellaneous downloadable resources

'Elevated rates of autism, other neurodevelopmental and psychiatric diagnoses, and autistic traits in transgender and gender-diverse individuals' by Varun Warrier *et al.* (2020): www.nature.com/articles/s41467-020-17794-1.pdf.

Autistic Self-Advocacy Network, National Center for Transgender Equality and National LGBTQ Task Force joint statement on the rights of transgender and gender non-conforming autistic people: https://autisticadvocacy. org/wp-content/uploads/2016/06/joint_statement_trans_ autistic_GNC_people.pdf.

Just Listen: Affirming Strategies for Supporting Gifted Transgender Youth By Paul J. "PJ" Sedillo, Ph.D., Rebecca Niederlander, and Orion: www.nagc.org/sites/default/files/ Publication%20PHP/bonuscontent/Transgender%20 and%20Gifted%206-21.pdf.

Trans Inclusion Schools Toolkit: Supporting trans, non-binary and gender questioning children and young people in Brighton & Hove educational settings: https://mermaidsuk. org.uk/wp-content/uploads/2019/12/AllsortsYouthPro-ject-Trans-Inclusion-Schools-Toolkit-Sept-18.pdf.

National Center for Transgender Equality *Fact Sheet on U.S. Department of Education Policy Letter on Transgender Students*: https://transequality.org/sites/default/files/ ED-DCL-Fact-Sheet.pdf.

Families in Transition: A resource guide for families of transgender youth by Central Toronto Youth Services (CTYS): https://ctys.org/wp-content/uploads/CTYS-FIT-Guide-2020-English-1.pdf.

Where to buy gender-affirming gear

Here are a few reputable companies that sell chest binders in various sizes and styles: www.gc2b.co and www.under-works.com.

You can find form-fitting clothing for transgender girls at the **Rubies** website here: www.rubyshines.com. And by searching **LeoLines** on Etsy.

Learn all about gaffs, which is a form of underwear used for tucking, from **Gender Gear** here: www.gendergear.ca/pages/all-about-gaffs.

Point of Pride offers the Transgender Surgery Fund, a Free Chest Binder Donation Program, a Free Trans Femme Shapewear Program, an Electrolysis Financial Support Program, a Hormone Replacement Therapy (HRT) Access Fund, and other community-building support initiatives for trans youth and adults. You can find more information at www.pointofpride.org.

Books for children

I am Jazz by Jessica Herthel and Jazz Jennings
It Feels Good to Be Yourself: A book about gender identity by
    Theresa Thorn
Jacob's New Dress by Sarah and Ian Hoffman
Julián Is a Mermaid by Jessica Love
My Princess Boy by Cheryl Kilodavis
Red: A crayon's story by Michael Hall

The Boy & the Bindi by Vivek Shraya

They, She, He: Easy as ABC by Maya and Matthew Smith-Gonzalez

Books for teens and young adults

Before I Had the Words: On being a transgender young adult by Skylar Kergil

Beyond Magenta: Transgender teens speak out by Susan Kuklin

George by Alex Gino

Gracefully Grayson by Ami Polonsky

Some Assembly Required: The not-so-secret life of a transgender teen by Arin Andrews

Sorted: Growing Up, Coming Out, and Finding My Place (A Transgender Memoir) by Jackson Bird

Memoirs written by parents of transgender kids

Found in Transition: A mother's evolution during her child's gender change by Paria Hassouri MD

I Promised Not to Tell: Raising a transgender child by Cheryl B. Evans

Love Lives Here by Amanda Jette Knox

Raising Ryland: Our story of parenting a transgender child with no strings attached by Hillary Whittington

Soar Adam Soar by Rick Prashaw

Straight Expectations: The story of a family in transition by
  Peggy Cryden
The Bold World: A memoir of family and transformation by
  Jodie Patterson
The Unfinished Dollhouse: A memoir of gender and identity
  by Michelle Alfano
Uncommon Girls by Carla Grant
*What We Will Become: A mother, a son, and a journey of
  transformation* by Mimi Lemay

Advocacy resources

Human Rights Campaign advocates for equality on many levels, has a robust resources section and, if you live in the United States, you can narrow down to information in your state. www.hrc.org.

Global Action for Trans Equality (**GATE**) campaigns globally for trans, gender-diverse, and Intersex equality. You can find more information at www.gate.ngo.

Index